I0620662

LOSING WEIGHT NATURALLY

SEEKING HAPPINESS INEXPENSIVELY

RAHAB KIMANI

Losing Weight Naturally
Copyright © 2025 by Rahab Kimani

Library of Congress Control Number: 2025904943

ISBN
978-1-964488-96-7 (Paperback)
978-1-964488-97-4 (eBook)
978-1-964488-95-0 (Hardcover)

TABLE OF CONTENTS

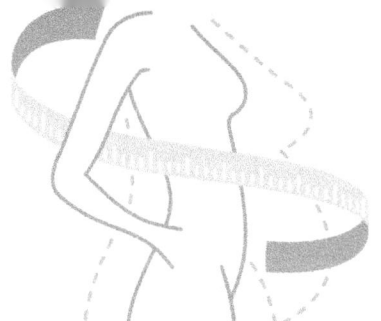

LOSING WEIGHT

The purpose of writing this book is to encourage those who wish to lose weight naturally to achieve that goal. It's to motivate them to do what they already know. We all know that the secret to losing weight is diet and exercise. Therefore, it's not even a secret because it was revealed centuries ago. But why do some people still have a weight problem? Why do other people still decide to have weight-loss surgeries and accept to pay thousands of dollars for those risky procedures? Because the secret of diet and exercise is easier said than done. **That's where I come in, to encourage the people who feel like it's hard to lose weight, to feel like it's possible and to know for sure that they can do it.**

Sometimes we all want to sit there and do nothing because it may be fun to do so. Sometimes we are tired and other times we are sick, but most of the time we just want to watch television, use the computer, iPad, or Smartphone. Whatever it is that causes people not to want to get physically active is what I am trying to change. It's all in the mind, so I'm trying to get them to change their mindset by welcoming them into my mind to let them see my thought process and how I manage to lose weight fast. I am trying to help them know that they can diet and exercise without feeling as if it's a punishment. **It is the OBLIGATION of dieting and exercising that causes people not to want to do it.** I would think that the obligation causes the rebellion. In my case, I no longer feel the obligation. I have set my lifestyle in such a way that dieting and exercising is part of my life, especially exercising.

The main reason why I decided to focus on my personal experiences while writing this book especially concerning weight loss is that there are many facts that I have only composed without necessarily consulting science, and I believe are true because I relied on them during my weight-loss journey and other journeys I have gone through while in the process of pursuing happiness. I wish to share my experiences that I underwent which resulted in my success, and thus my conclusions.

My decisions to carry out the actions that led to my achievement of my goal weight were as a result of my insight and readiness to finally shed the weight. Besides relying on the knowledge I had already acquired over the years, I also relied on the knowledge that I attained from all the experiments I tried during my weight-loss journey that resulted in my accomplishment of my dream weight. I was surprised at how much knowledge just flows in when the door is opened. The most important time for me was the eye-opening moment when I made the decision to get my body back but the most interesting thing was knowing that most of the knowledge I needed to lose weight had been here with me the whole time. All I had needed to do was **just put it into practice.**

MY WEIGHT STORY

I had always looked slim and fine for so many years, but I had taken it for granted and hadn't realized that some people struggle with weight. How could I complain about being a size 8, 10, or 12? I felt in control of what size I wanted to be. It was when I had my first child that I, too, gained weight. **I was so much in denial that I kept telling myself that the weight would be gone in a short time.** I didn't even take the initiative to buy new, bigger clothes right away. What would the bigger clothes be for if I was going to lose weight soon? Almost a year passed by, and I resumed going to church regularly but I was still in denial about clothes not fitting me. One day my close friend told me that I looked as if I was still pregnant, especially while I wore a dress I used to wear while I was pregnant. It was not a maternity dress, but I sure liked to wear it then because it was comfortable. I felt so horrible that I knew it was time to hit the mall and buy some fitting bigger clothes. Size 16 was the right size and to make the size seem worse, those new clothes began to get tight right after I bought them. So, I was actually a size 18 but never admitted it. What I admitted was that I was 5 feet and 7 inches tall and weighed 210 pounds.

It was almost time to go visit my family in Kenya and I knew they would be shocked to see me. Their shock would get in the way of our socializing, and I was not ready for that. How could I face them that way while they had seen me last when I looked fantastic wearing my size 12 wedding gown some 4 years before? I had to do something about it. I changed my diet and started exercising. **It was good to have an incentive to lose weight,** and that was, going to Kenya. I had two months before the trip, so I didn't have much time to waste. I began to order salads for lunch like some other people at work had been doing. I did not know I could enjoy salads so much. I also started making my own fruit salads and packing them as lunches and snacks. For lunch I would add a little rice to the fruit salad to make it more satisfying. But I would still get hungry quickly, so I would eat more salad 4 hours later. When I would get home in the evening, I would go outside to run for 10 minutes and then much later I would eat a good balanced supper. As the trip approached, I got so dedicated to the exercise that I started running in the mornings before preparing to go to work and still kept my evening running routine. By the time I flew to Kenya, I had lost 10 pounds, and my size 16 clothes could fit me comfortably. But my family, friends and relatives were still shocked to see the big me. I told them I had lost some weight, and I was surely glad I had because they would have been more shocked if I hadn't. When I told my dad how I had eaten salads for lunch for 2 months, he said, "That is called starving". So, I knew better not to do that again.

There in Kenya I did not have a personal car. I relied on public means of transportation. Therefore, I was walking more and more every day around my town as I ran my errands. Sometimes I would walk with my child in my arms or back. I'll never forget one day in Nairobi City when I had to carry my two-and-a-half years old daughter, plus a heavy bag for a long distance just to catch a Minivan to a Nairobi estate, Zimmerman. I could not believe how exhausting that experience and other such experiences that I encountered around that time could be. But when I went back to my town, Nakuru, everyone at home commented that I was losing weight. How could that be when I had been eating so much of everything I had missed? I discovered that **walking could help lose weight,** so I stopped complaining about being tired of walking. I began to walk with a positive attitude and excitement of possibly losing more weight by the time I'd return to the states where walking was almost a "never" for me.

When I returned to the US, I got so many **looking-good compliments which gave me the motivation to lose even more weight or maintain that weight in order to maintain my glory.** My friends were amazed by my weight loss. It had only been 7 weeks since I left, and I can now say that going to Kenya helped me think twice about how dormant I had been in the USA due to availability of a car and lack of insight. But just one week after my return, I discovered I was pregnant. Therefore, I began to balloon again slowly. By the time I was 4 months pregnant, I was told that I was expecting twins. I could not believe it, but I was very excited. Some months later I became so big that my friend still tells me to this day how big I looked then. What I know to this day is that I felt very heavy. By 28 weeks, I developed complications and delivered my twin boys early. Even though it was a depressing experience, I was glad that the weight was off my shoulders. It was tough dealing with a caesarian section wound and 2 preemies in the Neonatal Intensive Care Unit (NICU). But one thing I knew was that I was going to lose weight. I knew that for sure because I had felt how it was to carry heavy weight, and I had not felt good during pregnancy both physically and emotionally especially when friends had told me I was too huge. I had dragged myself during pregnancy and experienced how weight could interfere with my speed of doing things in the kitchen or elsewhere. I had not liked the feeling of being the biggest person in the crowd and I had not felt any beautiful when friends had said I was big. I wondered what they expected with twin pregnancy. There was nothing I could have done to help my weight and my appearance at that time. Even after delivery, I could not have done anything about my weight due to that major surgery, the caesarian section. I learned that **even though people judge you when you are overweight without knowing what you are going through and what has resulted in your weight, they can still judge**

you for being huge even when they can clearly see the cause of it.

My excitement was beyond limit just to know that I was healing, and I would be able to do something about my unhealthy weight. I had to lose it quickly and I was determined not to waste any more time. **I did not want to carry the weight around for some years and then lose it when I would turn forty or some other older age. I had to lose it while I was still 33 so that by 40, I would have enjoyed my smaller size for 7 good years. I would have enjoyed my new beauty for 7 extra years.** I failed to understand why I had carried around my weight for 3 years since my daughter was born. Instead of losing weight, I had replaced my closet with bigger clothes. I think I had not seen the importance of losing weight. I had been contented with being big and I had become used to my big size, but I wish I had not. I do not know why I had not felt hurt by the loss of my previously awesome figure and most of the attention I had been used to getting. I had flowed with the happenings. **I was not aware of my declining beauty and my mind was completely blank when it came to my looks. But I could surely feel the negative difference in the way people treated me.** The same people that had known me when I was slimmer were telling me how they had thought I was beautiful those days when I had less weight. Some even confessed to me that they had had a big crush on me when I was thinner. They were nice enough to avoid telling me that I was now fat, and the crush had vanished. But surely, I just do not know why their comments never caused me to want to lose weight. I think I was emotionally down. The job I used to have was emotionally draining and I was still raising my daughter. I do not understand what caused me to be so blind, but I am glad I finally saw the light while expecting my twins. I realized the importance of shedding weight and I cannot cry over spilt milk any longer. I move forward and do what I should have done years ago. It is better late than never.

While my babies were in the NICU, an hour away from our house, I would go to the hospital every other day and my husband went there every day while at work since he worked at that same hospital. I had realized that when I had gone there every day, I had not healed as fast as when I had given myself some rest, both physically and emotionally. I would wake up in the morning as early as my husband would wake up in order to ride with him and get to the hospital in time for him to clock in at work and I would stay at the hospital almost all day long, waiting for him to clock out and give me a ride back home. Meanwhile, I would hold my babies, go to the mothers' room for pumping breaks, and go to the cafeteria for lunch. The distance to the restroom and cafeteria from the NICU gave me a head-start in my walking plan. There was no wasting time, as getting busy quickly was not an option. Walking from the parking lot to the hospital just 5 days after my surgery was not my choice but my responsibility. I had to see my babies. Even the distance from my hospital room to the NICU before I had been discharged had not been short since it had only been 1 to 4 days since the surgery. **But I had been glad that I had begun to exercise through those painful but necessary walks.**

One month passed by and I felt strong enough to walk farther. **So, I started walking around my neighborhood for 30 minutes every day in the evenings.** I would walk slowly and as time went by, I increased my speed. I could not run yet because I wasn't all well, but I was longing for the time I would be able to run. My babies were still in the NICU by that time. On the days I would go to see them, I would end up taking only 2 meals a day not because I wanted to but because that was what my schedule allowed me. I was already well enough to drive myself to the hospital, and I now had flexibility. I would take my breakfast at around 10 am and get to the NICU at noon. I would hold my babies and do the other important things such as having pumping breaks, until 4 pm. But I still had to pick up my daughter from school at around 5 pm. It would make me feel guilty to think that I could stop somewhere to eat, because she was also hungry. **Therefore, I would stay hungry until I would pick her and we'd go home to eat together.** The drive from the hospital to her school was almost 1 hour, but the drive from her school to our home was 5 minutes. That's how come **I didn't have an option to eat on the road but I embraced the situation because it was working to my advantage.** After supper at home, I would leave her with her father shortly so that I would go outside to walk. **Whenever I came back from my**

walk, I would not eat any more food. I didn't even have much appetite. I thought the loss of appetite was as a result of the medication I was taking at the time and also the long hours I was spending at the hospital and the emotional distress caused by the condition of my babies. Every weekend, friends would be shocked at how fast I was losing weight, and they would ask me what I was doing. **Some could not believe me when I told them I was only walking and eating less.** Some even said that I had probably had a lap band, gastric bypass surgery, or something like that.

By the time my babies came home, they were two months old and from then on, I did not have time to walk every day but sure enough **I had more exercise in the house while raising them than I ever needed.** Twins, oh yes, they are exciting double blessings, and double smiles, and double work too. I could not get time to sleep. I was constantly running around the house while washing their dishes, trying to pump some milk, diaper changes, dealing with their refluxes, the feedings and the crying and still picking my daughter from preschool, all without help. In the mornings, I would pack my twin boys and my daughter in the car, and we would all go to drop her off, and in the evenings, I would pack the boys in the car again and we would go pick her up. And when we got back home, I would unload everyone and begin working afresh since I still had to raise my daughter and give her all she needed as a child regardless of how much I had given her brothers. Sometimes I would park the car in the garage and before I would unload them,

I would stay there for a minute, not willing to get out and face my evening. Other times it would be feeding time for everyone upon arriving home. Just knowing that my daughter would be so hungry and had to wait for her brothers to feed since they would be hungrier, and both crying was stressful enough. Sometimes I, too, would be hungry but of course I would not have anything before the children. I got used to feeling hungry without immediately responding to my hunger. I learnt that **it is possible to continue with life while hungry without collapsing from that hunger.** And that is one of the biggest lessons I learnt that prepared me for my weight-loss journey. But with time I also learnt how to manage my time to avoid that situation of having everyone hungry at the same time.

After several weeks we employed a lady to help us with some of the work. She could not handle it for too long either, so she left six weeks later and all by myself again I faced all my work and my fatigue. My husband was the breadwinner, so he would work most of the time but there were days he would sleep with the babies to help with feeding, especially when I was on the verge of losing my soul. He did what he could, and I did not expect any more help than he gave, but what was left on my plate was enough to drain my weight fast and that was, let's say, a good thing. **I learnt that when work is too much for me, I should embrace it if losing weight is one of my goals.**

By the time my babies were 5 months old, I would wear a size 10, all the way from size 18. With all the weight loss, there also went my whole closet. Some clothes were not exciting to lose so I altered those and hit the mall for a whole new closet. Even that was not very easy but it was surely too much fun. **Walking around the mall and trying on clothes was a whole new weight-loss program.** Sometimes I would take my babies with me, and it took quite a bit of calories unloading them and loading them back in the car as many times as the number of stores I went to. Whatever took away the most weight was probably their heavy duo stroller that I had to keep unloading and loading back in the car. It was energy draining but I embraced it because it helped me maintain my weight for some time. Besides the manual work, **going to the mall really motivated me to work on my figure in order to comfortably fit in the clothes I was trying on and it also motivated me to maintain my weight in order to avoid losing my new clothes that I so loved.**

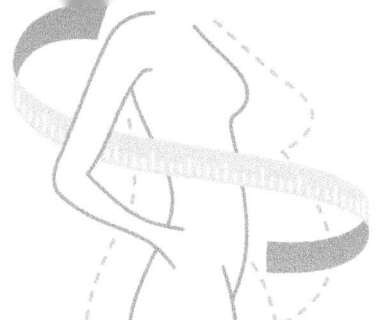

MAINTAINING GOAL WEIGHT

It had been about 10 months since the babies were born. The shopping spree had been over, the babies had grown bigger, and the work had become less. My appetite was back and most of the stress was gone. Summer was back and so did the parties. Picnics at the parks, eating from the patios of some fancy restaurants, all back. The babies could sit outside, so why not enjoy the outdoor world? Cold sodas and snack sales outside our church were back. The cookouts, barbecues, and all the summer fun that involved a lot of eating were back in full swing. There were many birthday parties at people's houses and party places, and ice cream and cakes and such desserts were there. Life was good but only one threat: gaining the weight back. That's when my discipline kicked in. **The question of what was more important between maintaining my weight and letting myself get carried away by the moments was necessary.** Getting carried away was fun and important but maintaining my weight was important to me too.

I kept my scale close by. Weight comes slowly and goes slowly. People don't notice that they are getting bigger until they have added quite a bit of weight, unless they are weighing themselves. **To avoid getting surprised, I weighed myself once every week.** That way, I would never add more than 5 pounds and fail to notice. I never let myself go beyond 5 pounds before I would begin exercising hard and dieting to lose it. **It's the 5 pounds that increase and become 10 and more and then the clothes fail to fit. Then the work of losing it becomes overwhelming and may cause despair and a weight problem for years.** I am determined to never lose my size 10 and 12 closet. The size 12 clothes are loose enough to be altered. I should have waited to lose all the weight I had to lose before buying any new clothes to make sure they would never be loose. But anyway, I still had to dress every step of the way, so no regrets.

I joined a gym membership where I worked out once a week at most. **At the gym I attended a dancing class that lasted one hour every Tuesday morning.** After an hour, I would feel assured that I had maintained my weight for the next one week considering how tired the dance made me feel. But it was so much fun to dance, and I imagined it took away a lot of calories. It was also my way of going out to meet other ladies and getting away from my house on a Tuesday morning while the babies bonded with their daddy during his morning off from work. That was my 'me-time'. Some weeks I didn't even make it to the gym because either my husband would have the mornings planned for or I would have to take the babies for their appointments.

But when I couldn't go to the gym, I did something in the house. For example, I tried to do some sit-ups in order to work on my weakest point, my abs. I wished I could do more, but I was still very busy running around the house chasing my babies since, by then, they were already busy moving around trying to 'fix' everything.

As they grew older, my babies were getting heavier, so I continued lifting weights in the house in the name of putting them into their cribs, highchairs or other such responsibilities. To this day, I still do my kitchen chores and that's enough to maintain my weight even when I eat enough during the week, and a little more than enough during the weekends. I am waiting for the time I'll go back to work and that's when the challenge of dieting harder will kick in because if I sit all day at the desk, my exercise program will be gone. But one thing I know for sure is that **procrastinating is the worst thing I can ever do to myself when it comes to maintaining weight.** The idea of planning to exercise tomorrow or next week or next month instead of today is the worst. My tomorrow never comes but the world is still revolving and with every passing day is another day of adding weight or carrying around the present excessive weight. By the time I realize that I've been adding weight, I am already fat. 'With every pound I add, I lose confidence and self-esteem worth one pound'. After a chunk of time has passed, I start feeling as if I am not pretty. I hope that I will never procrastinate again. I will continue to fit my exercise time into my daily routine.

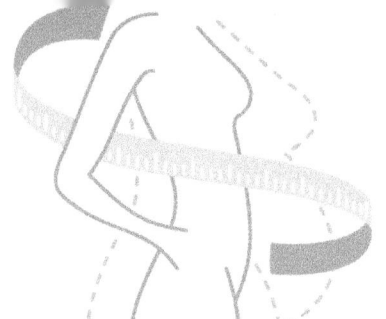

EXERCISING

Working out is not something so special. It should be second nature. The idea of dressing up in a tracksuit and sneakers does not always have to be the norm. I can do some exercises in my pajamas if need be. It does not have to be done at a specific time or a specific place such as the gym. Setting up a specific time and making exercise seem to be very special is what brings laziness that causes me to abandon the whole exercise plan altogether. **I have learned to work out as I go on with my daily chores.** For example, since one of my boys used to cry when I would leave his room before he would sleep, I'd stay in his room and do my Ab crunches until he'd sleep. That's time I could have been wasting if I would just have been sitting there doing nothing. He had even gotten used to my exercise in his room and it did not distract him from falling asleep.

Usually, when I watch the news or my favorite programs on TV, I slowly do my sit-ups on the ball without getting bored since my mind is on TV and not on my exercise. I have realized that it is so difficult to exercise on that ball when I am not entertaining myself. Nobody likes boredom and it's not interesting to put my mind on my exercise. That is why I had even joined the dancing class so that I could entertain myself with music and dance until I'd sweat. These kinds of distractions were more important to me when I first began to exercise, when exercise seemed to be a waste of my time. As time goes by, exercise seems like a way of life and avoiding it seems like a waste of an opportunity to feel good and become healthier.

When I never used to exercise, the imagination of working out used to be woeful. But now that I've been exercising, I feel wonderful, and I am glad I do so, and I wish to do more of it. When people ask me what I am doing to lose weight, I say, "diet and exercise" and most people say they don't like to hear the word "exercise". Maybe they expect to hear some other magic that I do to lose weight, but **exercise is the magic. It's a fun kind of magic if I perceive it to be so.**

Walking outside in the name of exercising to lose weight can be boring to imagine. So, whenever I did not want to walk when my babies were younger, I would tell myself that I was just going to take a break from my busy house. I would imagine leaving my babies with their dad for 30 minutes, and the imagination of not having to be in the house for that much time would encourage me to get out of the door. It was so much fun to walk. Experiencing the breeze and having time to be alone to think about anything without being distracted was something I could not find in my house. Walking time was the only time to meditate, and despite the rain, the sun, and the cold, there was something so spiritual about it. Something so healing of my mental stress during that particular time was definitely a treasure. Sometimes it was my time to cry out all my distress and other times it was time to fantasize my fantasies. After all that fun, I would arrive home some ounces lighter. What a big reward? It was just a win-win situation.

I know it's difficult to gain a whole pound overnight and the opposite is also true. It's hard to lose a whole pound at once. So, **what matters is the ounces. A single ounce will increase and become a pound sixteen ounces later.** So, whenever I want to lose weight, I consider every single activity as a weight-loss plan. We've all been told that parking our cars far away from the building is better than parking closer, but I had not taken the advice seriously. It was when I was working hard to lose weight that I started parking far away. I considered the possibility of losing a single ounce very important. It is definitely obvious that when I parked farther, I lost more ounces than when I parked closer, all other factors held constant.

The walks that I used to take in the evenings were not always very easy to take. Sometimes it would rain when I was far from getting home, and all I could do was just continue walking. There was absolutely no place to take shelter. I would arrive home wet, but **the mess was always fixable.** I used to encourage myself by saying, "I am not going to dissolve in the rain like salt". At some point, I began to put a shower cap into my pocket to protect my hair from wetness in case it would rain. Other times it would get too cold, and I had to keep walking. I would run in order to heat myself up a little. By then I had healed from my surgery. Running is more effective than walking–if the amount of time in both cases is the same–but it's also harder to run. **To make sure that I ran, I'd walk for a while and then I'd run until I'd get exhausted, and then I'd walk again. That way, I did not feel the obligation to run because I knew I could stop any time I wanted to.**

Just knowing how cold it would be sometimes was likely to keep me in the house. So, I would encourage myself by wearing a track jacket that was warm enough, before beginning my walk. But most of the days I would end up removing it and tying it around my waist. **It was not what I would go through that was hard enough to keep me from walking; it was the imagination of it.** So, getting out of the house was what really mattered. Once out there, I was strong enough to endure the outside conditions. So, every day I had to challenge my laziness and irrational thoughts and all of that was only about opening the door and starting to walk. The rest was okay as long as **I had my sneakers and socks on to protect my feet.** The first days I walked with the wrong shoes and came back with blisters.

One day I had to take off my shoes and walk back home barefooted, and that was painful. Another day I wore my sneakers but did not wear socks and I formed a painful cone. The hardest experience was one day when I ate and immediately started walking and halfway through the walk, my stomach began to hurt, and I could not walk anymore. The sharp pain on the right side of my stomach led me to think that I would call for help but I had forgotten my phone that day, so I took shortcuts and slowly walked back home in much pain.

It was very important for me to **carry my phone during the walks.** That gave me some confidence and even though my neighborhood seemed safe, there was always the thought of abduction. My husband used to emphasize the need to go with the phone every day but after I stopped walking frequently, he said he would rather not see me walk anymore considering the abduction cases on TV every now and then. I can still walk once in a while, but now I'll have even more challenges to overcome, including convincing my husband that God will protect me. If someone cannot walk outside, walking on the treadmill is okay too but I personally prefer to walk outside.

Gym membership seems to be expensive and only for those who have a lot of money to spare. But I think it's for anybody who wishes to have it. I found a deal that was inexpensive, and **I think most gyms have some inexpensive offers** too. I wanted the cheapest offer to let me just put my foot into the door and exercise. All the other extras, I felt were too much to ask for. The dancing class helped me realize what I could do at home by myself. I now know I can do ab crunches, and those words were not even in my vocabulary at first. I also know how to use the exercise ball, and I know I can dance for a whole hour even at home without thinking that I'm crazy. I had those resources such as the ball, the music, and the floor before I joined the gym, but I never knew how to use them. Even though I no longer have to go to the gym, I learned a lot from it. **What matters now is what the gym taught me rather than what it gave me.**

What I did to shed my weight was what I could do during that period of time and I used whatever resources were available to me at the time. Other people can do other different things and use other resources or services, but **it's not about what one can do; it's about what one is doing**. I will continue to work with what I have. Someday I may get motivated to buy a bicycle or the exercise equipment they advertise on T.V. but **it's not buying the equipment that's important, it's using the equipment. It's getting up and starting to exercise that matters most.** The process of exercise is always fun for me. But sometimes it's hard to begin exercising. For example, it's not swimming that is boring for me to do. It's going to the pool and getting wet the first one minute that is hard to imagine. **Let's all overcome the first few minutes of the exercise process, and in the end, we'll be glad we did it.**

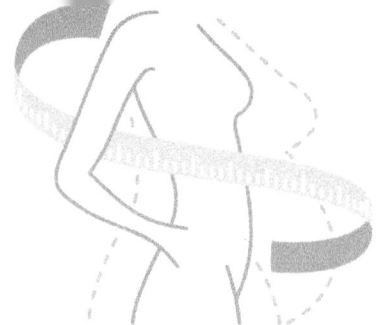

DIETING

Food is very delicious, especially to food lovers like me. Some foods are irresistible. It feels good to go to a buffet restaurant and binge on everything I've been missing. Once in the restaurant, I can eat all the courses of the meal especially the desserts without limitation. How can I leave behind a key lime pie, a pumpkin pie, or a French silk pie? If I could find them all in one restaurant, I would not dare to leave any uneaten. How about the juicy steak from the steak house, and the baby back ribs with barbecue sauce over them, with some French fries, fresh buttered dinner rolls, corn bread or rice or anything on the side? All are very yummy, but not a good idea to have them all. For me, I know I can eat them all by having a little bit of everything, so **why would I go to a buffet restaurant or the steakhouse to tempt myself when I'm trying to lose weight?** There is no need.

My family and I used to go out to eat almost every Sunday, but now I choose other kinds of entertainment rather than going to restaurants. It is fun to do other things too and I don't feel like I am missing the restaurants the way I used to. **It's all in the mind.** I make sure that there is very delicious food at home so that going home from Church is a fun option too. It's better than when I never used to have food in the fridge on Sundays and my husband would dread going home and waiting for me to cook while he was hungry, and I would absolutely not want to go cook while hungry either. So, the only option would be to eat out. That is not the case anymore. Even on Saturdays I cook nice food and now my husband no longer brings home the yummy Chinese food that I used to binge on. We can still go out to eat because **it's not eating out that causes weight gain. It is the frequency of binging.** If I binge twice or thrice a week, I am more likely to gain weight than if I only binge once a month.

Sometimes even home food will cause great weight gain if binged on, but I am so less likely to binge on home food. I cannot binge on it because I can keep it in the fridge and still eat it later, unlike food away from home that I will leave behind and have no access to later if I want it. What I am likely to do at home is snack too much. It's entertaining to take some hot cocoa with some African doughnuts known as 'Mandazis' or some cake or my signature home baked banana bread that I am known for. Sometimes I'll have banana bread and the doughnuts in my fridge at the same time and it's hard to choose what I want to snack on and I end up choosing both. That is way too much sugar. And don't forget the 2 teaspoons of sugar added into the cocoa. Sometimes when I snack on doughnuts, I just don't wish to use anything but soda. That's weight right there. To avoid this problem, whenever I want to lose weight, **I will not make any doughnuts and banana bread, and I will not buy soda.** That will kick out the starch, the cocoa and its sugar from my dining table and keep the sodas in the grocery store instead of my pantry. It's amazing how many calories I let stay in the fridge, pantry, or the store by not making the homemade snacks. **If I need snacks, I take fruits or a glass of milk.** I often wish that there are some doughnuts in the fridge but the fact is that they are not there.

It is the availability of food that keeps me eating. Sometimes I will not cook enough food during weekdays just on purpose. I will have enough for my husband and my children but not for me. I will find myself eating some lettuce and tomatoes and some sandwiches and wishing I had cooked, but the fact remains that I had not. Then after some days I'll cook because I don't want tomatoes any more. I'll have food, but the good thing is that I'll have dieted the past few days on vegetables, fruits, boiled eggs, and milk. Sometimes I buy my daughter's favorite cereal and not my favorite. So, during breakfast I either eat her favorite cereal, which I don't usually do, or just take milk with a small piece of bread. The piece of bread is small because I don't even like bread without some spread anyway. Some mornings, I just take only milk and wait for 2 hours when it's time for lunch and then I'll eat enough. The good thing is that I never even once feel like I'm depriving myself of anything because there is nothing I see and wish to eat and not eat. If it's not in my fridge, how would I struggle with temptation? I don't even feel bad that the banana bread is not in my fridge because I know the ingredients are in my pantry. It's just a matter of baking it, and where is the time to bake? I'd rather watch T.V. or go for a stroll in the mall buying nothing. But when my family misses the snacks, I'll bake and resume eating them, but I'll have lost my five pounds by then anyway. Then I'll get invited again to a party at someone's house. It's yet another time to binge on the barbecued meat and the fun snacks. But I have learned that even there I can avoid eating too much. **I only eat the most tempting foods.** Why should I eat food that is not so delicious when all it is going to do is cause me to add more weight? If the flat tasting food is on my plate, it's already served. So, even if I don't eat it, nobody else can have it and so I can do whatever I want to do with it, including trashing it, without making any difference to the economy.

There was a time when I could not trash food. Not when kids were dying of hunger in Africa. I would even eat my daughter's leftovers to avoid trashing it. How could I let it go to waste? Not anymore. If my daughter does not want her food, it's either going back to the fridge for later or it's going straight to the trash can. Eating it for her is not saving the food because I already ate mine. It's just trashing it in my stomach because I do not need it in the first place. But if I have not eaten mine and she refuses her whole plate, I can probably eat hers, and in that case, I will not serve mine. Hers will be unused food that I can use as my supper, but not an additional meal in my stomach to cause me to add more weight or feel bad about myself.

Self-pity sometimes might hit someone when one is hungry as a result of food shortage or inability to afford it. But also, it does not feel good when there's a lot of food around someone if she can't have it because she is trying to lose weight. That's why I have to balance these emotions by having the food available to me in the pantry but not in ready form. Not in my fridge. **I also try to balance between food availability and unavailability.** If I have had delicious snacks for a while, it's okay not to have them for a while too. If I haven't gone to the restaurant for a while, it's okay to go there once in a while. If I have not binged on barbecued meat for some weeks, I can do so for once. If my sodas have been waiting for long in the fridge, it's ok to have one after a while. If I miss banana bread, it's ok to bake one after some weeks. That way, my lifestyle is not horrible and deprived. I don't even have to hit the gym several times every week whenever I have membership. If I have been working out for a while, it is okay to be a couch potato for once and enjoy the T.V. **The only problem is doing all the negative things frequently, consecutively, or always.** For example, if I go to a party on Saturday and binge, and the next day after church I go to a restaurant with friends and binge again, and then on Monday I go to a drive-thru restaurant and order a cup of coffee and breakfast burrito, and then I go to work and accept the donuts people bring, and at lunch I order a large burger and fries and soda or shake, and in the evening I eat some ice cream and cake or chew some snacks on my way home, then I eat a healthy meal at supper because I am on a diet, and then I lay on the couch because I'm tired and catch up with my TV shows before I go to bed, and do this Monday through Friday, I'll be asking for pounds. That's undoable by me forever. I'm determined never to go back to that kind of lifestyle. That's a weight gain program. I can't do that and not expect to be fat. I already did it and proved it years ago.

I used to snack every break time and on my way home to relieve my stress. Then one day a friend asked me, "Do you have to eat every break time?" I thought about it and realized that **I could do other fun things instead of snacking.** So, I started bringing books to read during breaks, and sometimes I enjoyed walking around the building or running a quick errand.

I used to hang around with food lovers like me and every break time we would go to the cafeteria to eat. We used to joke about it by saying that eating was the only entertainment we could get considering how short the breaks were. Some friends even liked food more than I did and they brought junk food to work and shared with the rest of us. **We would look for reasons to have parties and everybody would bring some food that wasn't even healthy and there would be a cake and ice-cream or some pies for dessert.** Sometimes we would just sit there and talk about food, restaurants, or recipes. All that interest in food caused weight gain on my part. It's a lifestyle I thought I could not change but I did. All the lunches with fellow employees at the restaurants are now gone and **I'm sure I'll not go back to that hobby of sampling restaurants** even when I start working.

I'll never forget how we used to go to our favorite buffet restaurant and try our best to get our money's worth of food at lunch time. We would go back to work feeling sleepy and lazy. **Birds of the same feather flock together and so do people with the same hobbies. Food lovers eat together and sometimes some hobbies are overdone. Influence plays a big part when it comes to eating.** If the people I hang out with eat more, why not me? But now I am aware that accepting to be influenced by friends to eat is not smart, so I can't flow so much with the current now and in the future. On the other hand, I've realized that **it is better to hang out with friends who don't eat much if losing weight is my priority.** One day I went to a fast-food restaurant with some friends and I ordered an extra-large burger which shocked them to a point that they started to talk about it in my presence. They were asking each other, "Can you handle that burger?" And they all said that they could not handle it. Before that day, I had handled it many times alone without knowing that it is relatively too big of a burger to eat in one sitting. But having friends around brought that fact to my awareness and since then I began to order the medium sized burger, and it still satisfies me. **Having people whose food portions you can compare to**

yours may help you know that what you eat may be too much. I have seen people at parties noticing that my plate is too overloaded when they compare it to theirs while others notice that their plates are too overloaded just by comparing them to mine or other people's. The ones with overloaded plates may be ashamed and begin to comment about their big portions in an effort to probably excuse themselves or just suck in the shame and sit down to tackle their own eating business.

The most important thing to know is that losing weight and keeping it off should not only be a limited time plan but a LIFESTYLE. Incorporating some habits that will never disappear is essential. Those habits should not be taken as punishment. Driving oneself to the edge by depriving oneself too much and feeling uncomfortable about it is probably what makes most people give up on their weight-loss plan or make others gain back their weight right after they hit their dream weight. They go back to their fun old lifestyle and eat what they have been missing and surely gain weight faster than they had gained it initially. I personally live a lifestyle that does not punish me or make me feel deprived. One of the things I do as part of my lifestyle is walk or run my daughter to school most mornings since the school she now goes to is very near to our home. That's some exercise I get without thinking that I'm getting it or without going out of my way to get it. The same kind of mentality should be applied to dieting by leading my life on a path with circumstances that promote healthy eating, and it all begins at the grocery store when choosing what food to buy. It is very important to buy healthy ingredients with which to prepare food, while still allowing myself to overeat occasionally in order to get a break from strict dieting. Having the freedom to overeat and the discipline to reduce the frequency of overeating is more liberating than beating myself with the guilt of overeating even once.

During the early days of my weight-loss plan, friends would see me filling up my plate at a Saturday night party and they would comment that I was lucky because the food never made me fat. What they did not know was that I would only eat as such during those parties. I would religiously go back to my diet on Monday. **Whatever made it easier to go back to my diet during weekdays was knowing that I could eat during the weekends if I wanted to.** There was hope of enjoying everything I wished at some point in time. **Prolonged dieting would have caused me to give up the discipline but when I set myself free to eat at the Saturday parties, it caused me to see some light at the end of the tunnel.** All I needed was patience for a few days and sometimes even during those weekend parties, I would decide to just skip the binge and keep my discipline. Postponing the freedom to eat too much food was rewarding too because I would not have to strictly diet during the weekdays the way I used to after binging during weekends. I could not imagine that after all we would eat sometimes during those parties, anybody would go to a drive-thru restaurant to order some fast-fried food the next day. **The mentality of setting myself free to overeat during weekends was more important to me when it was still difficult for me to part with food.** But nowadays, I don't miss the binging. All it does is make me too uncomfortable to enjoy the party. But if the party is too dull and causes boredom, then I'll enjoy the binge, and that's the bad option.

Since the days of losing weight till now when maintaining it, **I have always lived in a way that everything I eat or do is a better option than the alternative. Doing several things that lead to weight loss is a better way to lose or maintain weight than doing just one thing.** I have heard people advising others to eat a certain cereal, or weight-loss shakes, or drink a lot of water, or drink a certain tea or eat supper before 8pm. These ideas are all true but trying only one of them may not help much. For example, drinking a lot of water and eating the same amount of food as before might not change anything. Eating a certain cereal and maintaining all other eating habits might also not change one's weight. The weight-loss shakes are supposed to replace meals, so drinking these shakes and not skipping meals is worse than not drinking them at all. Those shakes can help you gain weight really fast if meals are not skipped because they are loaded with calories. The most important thing to do is to try everything that one has ever heard from anywhere or anybody. If some books say drink a lot of water, and others say eat before 8pm, and others say eat vegetables and fruit instead of rice, try all those ideas and you'll be surprised how effective this can be. **By the time you try all those things, you'll have changed your lifestyle without realizing it.** Sometimes I can't even say exactly what I did to lose weight because I tried everything that I knew. If I had heard that it helps, I did it. In short, what I did was change my lifestyle. This way, if some things did not work, others did. Sometimes it's even hard to tell what worked the best. To this day, when I open the fridge, **I choose water instead of juice to avoid the sugar. Other times I decide to do away with butter on my bread, and other times I pick up a supplemental shake for breakfast or lunch when I am not so hungry. That means I replace my meal with the shake but not have both my meal and my shake. When I can't resist the doughnuts for snacks, I sometimes take them as my lunch. This way, they are not extra snacks that I am eating on top of my lunch.** They are just some kind of lunch I'm eating. Eating the doughnuts for lunch is choosing to eat an unhealthy lunch and it may not be the best for the body but as far as losing weight is concerned, it's better than eating those doughnuts in addition to a healthy lunch assuming that the number of doughnuts to be eaten in both cases will be the same. Instead of having the doughnuts bring in some extra calories, it's better for them to be the only calories taken. **Replacing is the key.**

Since I like doughnuts with some soda, I'll open a can anyway and use it sparingly but as soon as the

doughnuts are gone, I'll trash the rest of the soda. It sounds like wastage but it's better for the sugar and the calories to stay in the trash can, than go to my body to do some damage. But the trashing discourages me from buying more soda. In the end, I find myself not having any soda and I end up just eating my doughnuts with other drinks that are healthier than soda. **Sometimes at breakfast I only take some fruit. I really like buttermilk with sugar but sometimes I just skip the sugar.**

When I am at the grocery store, I choose brown instead of white. I choose brown sugar, bread, crackers, rice, flour and cereal. Choosing healthy all the time is better than choosing yummy. But it is very important for you to know that I also buy white rice, flour and more because I want to have them at home and use them when I really don't want to use brown. Having only brown food at home means I only have the brown option all the time and that may bring to me some feelings of **obligation** due to lack of freedom. I like to know that I'm eating brown because I prefer it to white, but not because I must. Sometimes I mix brown with white or alternate them day after day while still making sure that brown days are more than white days. In the end, the white sugar gets used in baking. **Whether you like brown food or not, remember that your decisions to eat brown begin at the grocery store before they happen at home. If you don't like brown food and you don't at least attempt to buy some, it means that you therefore have a 0% chance of eating**

brown when you get home. So, whenever you are at the store buying the yummy white food you like, it is better to also buy some brown food even when you don't expect to eat much of it in order to give yourself a fraction of possibility to consume it some days when you feel the mood to break the norm of eating the same white food. Some days of eating brown food are better than none.

During meals' time, it's better not to add the sugar, the butter, the cheese, the ketchup and mustard, the dressing and mayonnaise and all the nice tasting condiments every time. I don't do away with them completely either. I use them sometimes, but I skip them as many times as I can. More than half of the time I can sacrifice living without them. I imagine tea lovers that have to have sugar in their tea all the time and I just can't imagine doing that to myself. Too much sugar can be unhealthy, but some tea or coffee drinkers add it to their tea about 3 times a day. Cheese is good but food with cheese every day can help add weight faster. **Sometimes I skip fried food. French fries are wonderful but sometimes I'll ask for the kids' size so that I'll still eat them but not too much. That's MODERATION. I eat everything I miss all the time but eat in moderation most of the time.**

If I like a certain food so much that I cannot stop eating it, then I will avoid coming face to face with it frequently. I cannot stress enough that dieting is not depriving oneself of some favorite foods, it's choosing healthy. The wish to eat healthily must

come from within and should never feel like a punishment. It's not a punishment in any way. One should feel from deep within oneself the desire to eat healthily in order to have a better life. It's rewarding and it's worth all the sacrifice. After all, you reap the benefits even in old age.

I came to realize that there are some very nice tasting foods in the salad restaurants. I never thought I could enjoy some cold food made of only salads. Some vegetable salad served with some chicken salad and a dessert of fruit salad can make a very delicious healthy plate of food. It's all in the mind when it comes to choosing the foods I think are delicious. I like hot restaurant foods, especially fried ones but I also have a side of me that can enjoy the salads, so why not buy salads sometimes? Not always, because hot foods are a must for me, but those days that I choose the salads are helpful. It's better "SOMETIMES" than "never".

We CRAVE what we eat, and the foods we've never seen or eaten, we don't even think about. If one has a certain food that one cannot resist and is therefore unable to lose weight, I would suggest avoiding that food for a long time. I, for instance, crave the African doughnuts but one thing I can't imagine is that most people around the world may not even know which doughnuts I'm referring to. How could I be missing this kind of food so much while others don't even know it? I would say, because I eat it. Others on the other hand crave so many other things that I don't know. Those foods are their main problem when it comes to weight, and they are none of mine. So, I would say **we have control over our cravings.** Before I came to America, I had neither eaten nor seen some foods such as burgers, pizza, Chinese food, Mexican food, Indian food and many more. Almost all foods in America were new to me and yet now, I say I am really craving foods I didn't even know for most of my life. It's all in the mind and we don't have to be pessimistic about overcoming our cravings.

At first, the **WITHDRAWAL SYMPTOMS of food are scary.** The hunger pangs are unpleasant, the headaches and dizziness and lack of energy seem like sickness. Even emotionally, self-pity and being easily irritated may seem like very bad experiences. **But as time goes by, one can heal and adjust to eating less.** I personally lost most of those severe symptoms. The body adjusted to eating less. While I was going through the hunger symptoms, I thought it was going to be a permanent condition. **I would have quit dieting at that point, but holding on paid off.** This experience still comes back after a weekend of freedom of eating or after holidays. The body seems to want me to continue with the amount of food intake I had on Saturday or Sunday at a party or restaurant. I deal with the symptoms on Monday and the body gets used to less food intake again. **It is the knowledge of the fact that the symptoms disappear with time that is the most important. That knowledge gives me patience in waiting for the bad time to pass since I know it gets better.**

There's a time when my son's nurse warned me about his weight. She kept telling me not to overfeed him and eventually I heeded her advice, and my boy lost weight. I realized that she was warning me and not that little baby because he didn't know any better than I. Furthermore, I was the one who was responsible for my baby's weight. Since then, I know that **I am the one to blame if any of my kids is overweight.** I am the one who buys the food they eat, and I am the one who cooks it and serves it to them and watches them eat it. When they grow older and fly away from my nest, that's a different story. When they go to school and are fed wrongly, it's still not their fault. Some systems somewhere are not right, and some bad choices of available foods have been made for them by someone other than themselves. I cannot point fingers at parents with overweight kids though, because I do not know the situations in their homes. In my situation, I overfed my baby because he was crying, and the milk was quieting him. If it quiets the baby, why not give him more? **There is always a reason why parents let kids overeat, but there is always a better option to their problems other than excessive food consumption.**

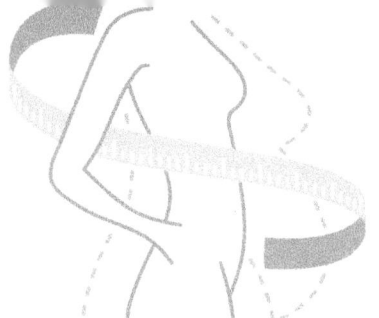

WEIGHING SCALE

There is no need to be obsessed with the scale. The scale does not make me any lighter and spending a lot of time on it does not help me emotionally especially when it reads to me the weight that I don't want to see. But if weighing every day is so necessary for the mind and motivation, then **weighing myself at the same time every day is likely to be more accurate than weighing myself at different times day after day.** For example, weighing in the morning every day before breakfast after bathroom use is likely to give me the actual weight of my body rather than my weight plus the weight of the food, the drinks, and the gas in the stomach. The weight I see on the scale in the morning is less than the weight I see on the same scale at night right before bed. So, someone may be discouraged by thinking that exercise and the diet are not working while in actual sense it may be just the wrong weighing time.

Even if the weighing is to be done once a week, still weighing at the right time is important because I might be led to think that I haven't lost any weight while I might have lost 3 pounds that are not showing on the scale because of the food, the drinks, and the hydration in the body. For example, if I weigh myself on Monday morning after bathroom use and before breakfast and weigh, let's say, 200 pounds, and in the course of the week I lose 3 pounds, then next Monday I weigh myself at bedtime and I'm still 200 pounds, I may give up on trying to lose weight. But if I had weighed myself in the morning before breakfast after the bathroom the second Monday, I would have come out of there dancing about the 3 pounds progress. So, weighing time is very important for the sake of motivation.

For so long, I've wanted to buy the digital weighing scale so that I can see the actual number as soon as I step on it. But when I recently bought one, it gave me inconsistent numbers and I took it back to the store. It could have been the brand I bought that was not perfect or just that particular scale. So, I'm stuck with the analog scale that can tell me the wrong weight when I don't make sure that the arm is initially at zero. The digital scale is good because it writes the number for me to see rather than have me try to count how many small calibrations the arm goes beyond the big calibrations. Sometimes when there is not enough lighting, I may have trouble seeing the exact calibration the arm is pointing at, and when I bend down to check, the arm points elsewhere. But the analog scale has the advantage of being more mechanical and may last long and may not give the wrong weight from being broken somewhere in its system like it happens with the digital scale sometimes. And now better innovations have introduced analog scales with bigger dials that enable one to see the calibrations more clearly. **So it's really up to the user to determine which weighing scale works perfectly.**

RELATIONSHIP WITH FOOD

It's unbelievable how difficult it is to stop overeating at first and so easy later. Saying goodbye to overeating favorite foods is like a breakup with a dear friend. It's surely a relationship breakup, the relationship between me and the food. Just like a relationship with a friend can be so addictive and seem like it will never end, a relationship with food is addictive too and seems like it will always be there. Breaking up with a friend is surely painful at first but with time it gets better and years later it's hard to imagine how much it had hurt. **Breaking up with food might not hurt as much as with a friend, but it surely is difficult, but it also gets better with time.** For me now, it gets to a point where I don't have to make food unavailable to avoid it. With time I am able to avoid eating it even when it's within my reach. And with time it sticks with me that I have to make healthy choices. Also with time, I stop craving snacks and it just becomes a lifestyle that I cannot imagine changing.

Just as effort is required to maintain a good relationship with a friend, **effort is also required to**

maintain a good relationship with food. When it comes to losing weight, you cannot be lazy in food preparation. Unless you have assistants to do the work, you've got to get up and go to the store to get healthy food. Or maybe nowadays you can just order groceries online. But even that requires an effort to do. Then you've got to spend time preparing the food in a way that will make it delicious in order to encourage yourself and your family to eat at home. You also have to be ready to wash the dishes after the meal and do some kitchen cleaning. You can either do all that work or you can just sit back and order some unhealthy ready food day after day or drive by a fast-food restaurant and skip all your cooking problems. When it comes to making food choices, it's your call. If you choose the easy way out, you unfortunately will not be helping with your weight issues much. Get up and work for your meals. Even fruits take energy to prepare unless you pick an apple, which by any means requires energy to wash and crunch. Losing weight by juicing is so popular nowadays. But when I imagine all the work and the time it may take to do it, I just pass the process. But the people who take their time to do it brag about the benefits they've gained from their hard work. Try the best you can to invest some of your energy in obtaining healthy meals. Choosing which restaurants to buy food from when you have to eat out is very important. **Some restaurants prepare healthy meals, but my problem with restaurant food is that I tend to eat a bigger portion of that delicious food than I eat at home.**

Breakfast is the most important meal of the day because it helps boost your metabolism. Some doctors say that we should eat our breakfast and not drink it. From what I have experienced, it's very important to avoid eating sweet food such as cake for breakfast. While eating a lot of sugar may keep me full for a long time, it's not a good idea to eat sweets while trying to lose weight. Hence, I may decide to reduce the amount of sugar by eating a small cake to satisfy my sweet tooth. However, **eating a small, sweet cake for breakfast causes me to feel so hungry so soon and the hunger may come with a headache when the sugar level goes down.** I may be forced to eat an early lunch, and thus an early supper and then I may be hungry before I go to bed and eat again. That means that I end up eating a whole extra meal on the day I eat cake or sweets for breakfast. I imagine that eating cake for breakfast causes the sugar level to go up and then down and I may spend all day trying to maintain the high sugar level by eating every now and then. And I may even spend the day craving sweets and obeying my cravings by eating more of those, and that only causes weight gain and other risk factors associated with eating excessive sugar.

The amount of food we consume is relative. What I call a small amount of food could be called a huge amount of food by someone else. What I may consider to be a huge amount of food may be just a snack to someone else. I have met so many heavy people who have told me that they don't eat a lot of food, but they do add weight. But I think that the amount of food they eat is not huge according to them because they probably have room for more but someone else might be unable to finish it. **Even when we think that the amount of food we eat is not much, it is important to eat a fraction of what we have been eating if 100% of that food seems to give us more weight than we need.**

Relationship with food is the most important thing when it comes to weight. In fact, I consider it to be more important than exercise. While some people have too much appetite, others have very little of it. Some friends have come to me complaining that they are too skinny, and they want to add weight. All I tell them to do is to eat harder. When I was a teenager and had this kind of problem, a friend came into my life and encouraged me to start with sweets and junk food, and eventually I was able to gain weight. But when I began to get some belly fat, that was the same friend who brought it to my attention. Years have passed since then and childbearing has come and gone. But as for my appetite, I have had more than enough since the birth of my first baby. **Sometimes I think it's the stress that came with the change of my lifestyle that caused me to turn to food as a way of comforting myself. Furthermore, I don't have as much time and freedom to entertain myself in a variety of ways like I used to. The kitchen and the T.V. are mostly all I've got. And that combination does not favor weight loss.**

As addictive as food can be to some of us, I have learned some tips that help me not to fall back to my old eating habits. First and most important, **I don't eat in front of the T.V. unless I don't care for either the food I'm eating or the program I'm watching. This helps me have a special eating moment without distractions.** When I used to eat while watching my favorite shows, I would finish my food without realizing that I ate too much. I would not even realize that the food was enjoyable because my mind was on T.V. Then later I would still have a craving for food because the eating experience had seemed to pass me by. I would have no memories of that wonderful eating experience, and I would therefore create another eating moment sooner than I needed to. Now that I enjoy my eating moments and still have memories of the experience later, I am able to go about other chores without craving for an eating moment because I just had it a few hours ago anyway. By the time I am hungry again, it's already time for the next meal which I am justified to have. Doing this kicks the snacking out of my entire day. In addition to enjoying the food and keeping that memory longer, **separating eating time from T.V. time helps my mind to know that I can enjoy the T.V. without chewing on something and vice versa. Watching T.V. while eating can get really addictive and can lead to a lot of weight gain.**

Of all the things that one may do to show signs of loyalty to food and a sign of no potential to lose weight quickly, hiding food is the number one thing that tells me how far one is from achieving their dream weight. Being so attached to the food and

enjoying the possession of it and having a lot of passion for it is a clue that you are addicted to it. The shame of eating everything that one has to eat in the open is an indication that one is eating too much, and will continue to eat that much as long as no one knows. The problem of doing that is that the food will help increase one's weight and the weight will not be hidden from the public. The most important thing to know is that hiding food is cheating no one but yourself because the public does not really care about how much you eat, but they are quick to judge you when you add weight. I would think that most people would not criticize someone based on their food portion as much as they would criticize someone based on their weight. Being true to the public about how much you eat is a step to being true to yourself. One of the reasons why people hide food is to avoid sharing. But the price we pay for not sharing food is gaining that extra ounce we would have shared with someone else.

Sharing food is another tip I have learned, and it does me a lot of good. When I was a food addict, I tended to keep my food to myself. My plate was mine and nobody was welcome to pick any of my favorite yummy food items from it. But now my attitude has changed. If someone wants my food, they can have it. They can even take the entire pot if they want. God will provide me with more and if I stay without food today, what's the big deal? I'll eat tomorrow anyway. This kind of attitude is one of the best things that I have acquired in an effort to maintain my weight because I feel as if the attitude is there to stay with me till I die. It's difficult to reach that point but once there, it's also difficult to go back to the same old selfish attitude. It's all in the mind.

Living with fear of ever being hungry used to cause me to stock up my freezer with too much food. I would stock up my fridge with cooked food and my counters with snacks. I would even stock up my car with snacks in case I would get hungry on the road. I would also take out food from parties in case I would miss it later. Sometimes I'd eat before I was hungry to avoid that moment when hunger would strike. The fear of hunger was overwhelming and caused me to eat more than I needed and therefore I added too much weight. I now still take some of those precautions to avoid hunger, but now I do it in a different way. For example, if it's almost lunch time and it's time to leave but I'm not hungry yet, I may put a sandwich in the car to eat when I get hungry. I will not eat it at home and carry it in my stomach, but putting it in the car will help me to avoid driving through a restaurant for some fast-fried food. **I schedule meals' time and foresee what is likely to happen when I get hungry and plan for it early instead of letting that time come and then make wrong decisions based on my hunger. When I go to a restaurant or party and pack some food to go home, I no longer just eat it as soon as I get some more space in my stomach to accommodate some extra food. That is food for the next meal or the next day. Eating just for fun can be unhealthy but eating**

to live can be more fun. I no longer live to eat but rather, I eat to live.

Another tip I have discovered that helps me eat less is preparing fruits and putting them close by as I eat my meals. Sometimes the beef stew and rice can be so delicious that I may be tempted to go back for more even when I know I shouldn't. To help me resist the temptation, I just pick up my bowl of fruits and my interest shifts from enjoying beef stew and rice to enjoying the sweet tasting fruits. By the time I am done with the fruits, the urge to eat more rice and stew is completely gone, and my stomach is full. All I feel like having is a glass of water, and I close the eating chapter. **But it is very important to prepare and serve the fruits ahead of time** because if I hope to get them ready after I eat my meal, chances are I will be too lazy to do so and I will prefer to just grab some more rice and stew because that's what I'm craving for anyway and if it's within my reach, why not? It is also very important to set the fruit next to me so that I won't have to get up after my meal to go for them. If I must get up, I'll head straight to whatever else I feel like eating. The reason why it is very important to place the fruit next to me is that when losing weight, the food I serve myself is less than enough and there is a very serious temptation to get some more of the same kind of food in an effort to fill up the stomach. The fruits, being there, will help me be able to cancel the trip to where the main pot of food is. When the fruits get to fill the stomach, fewer calories will be consumed and that will promote weight loss. **The fruits also help me eliminate the urge to drink sodas and juices that contain added sugar and other unhealthy ingredients. They also help me have the ability to peacefully skip the sweet desserts such as ice-cream and cake, and so, placing the fruit next to me while I have my meal saves me more calories than I can imagine.**

The fruits have done me a lot of good. When I am on a strict diet, I eat a lot of fruit-and-vegetable salad. I fill up a big bowl with some shredded lettuce or chopped celery. You'd think that the next thing would be to add dressing but, no, I just add my fruit salad. And the mixture of vegetable salad and fruit salad is delicious. On the side, I put one piece of chicken, like a thigh, and a slice of bread. Then I drink water and call it a well-balanced supper. The kinds of fruit I use for this kind of mixture are pineapple chunks and diced oranges. It's their juices that I'm interested in because they sweeten up the vegetable salad. If I don't have these kinds of fruit, for example if I just have apples or pears or peaches or plums or mangos, then I'll enjoy eating them separately without the vegetables. In that case, I'll need something for my vegetable salad. To avoid the dressing, I just use apple cider vinegar. Just a little bit of it will help alter the taste of the raw vegetables. **Whatever it is that I have to use for my vegetables, I try my best to make sure that dressing is not the option. It is my last resort and if I have to use it, I use the least amount that I possibly can and I make**

sure it's a low or no fat dressing. Italian dressing is my healthy choice of condiment.

There was a time I used to drink warm water with vinegar before bed, but the day I stopped using vinegar for a drink was the day I woke up with a serious heartburn. I suspected the cause was vinegar. But I've heard that vinegar is supposed to get rid of heartburn. I might have drunk a high concentration of it. Although it could have been something else, I felt the need to avoid vinegar to reduce the chances of heartburn in the future.

During the holidays, I get tempted to eat chocolate and other snacks that kids get on Halloween night. I have discovered a trick that helps me limit the intake of that chocolate and candy or other home snacks like cookies. **I no longer put a big bowl of snacks in front of me with the hope to stop eating when I get enough.** I realized that I always had a hard time stopping to eat especially chips, nuts, and popcorn. They have an addictive effect on me and once I start eating them, I can't stop till they are gone. I would end up eating more than enough, but not anymore. Now, I determine how much I need, serve it into a bowl and store the rest in the pantry. That way when I'm done eating my calculated portion, I will only wish I had more. This idea has helped me especially when I'm taking snacks to go. If I take 5 cookies to the car, I am sure I'll not eat more than 5 because the rest will be at home. Removing snacks is a strategy I use to limit myself from overeating them. Sometimes we don't plan to overeat, but food leads us into temptation and we find ourselves being carried away. Whether knowingly or unknowingly, overeating sweet or salty snacks makes me feel guilty afterwards. 'How could I let myself go uncontrollably?' **Putting those addictive snacks away beats this temptation with hope that "out of sight out of mind" policy will come into play.**

I realized that when I brush or floss my teeth right after eating, it discourages me from wanting to keep biting something extra. I've never tried this at a party but I'm yet to try. What I have done at a party is chew gum right after eating and that for sure helps reduce my interest in picking something to put into my mouth. I have also applied my lip moisturizer and lip gloss to keep me discouraged from drinking sodas or some wine. I have also used fruit as a way of snacking at parties after I have already eaten enough food. Every time I pass by food and feel like picking something, I pick fruits. They remind me that I am already full, and they surely satisfy my urge to eat extra food. That bowl of fruit salad could have been a couple of doughnuts.

I have learned that different lifestyles lead some people to eat differently, and changing the lifestyle just a little bit can change one's eating habits without struggling to do so. For example, I have realized that I don't like to eat at the drive-thru restaurants, and whenever I am out there running my errands, I tend to wait until I go home to eat. But when I don't go out, I may be tempted to eat more, especially when I have made interesting things to eat. Therefore, if I want to lose weight it's better for me to be out there than at home. Some other people like to eat fast food when they are out there. For those people, the best thing for them is to stay home where they don't have to be tempted to eat fast food. Eating food that is not very interesting may definitely be what causes one to eat less of it. It may be difficult to stay home or be out there just for the sake of avoiding eating what tempts you to eat too much of, but it may be possible to do so. When having a day off from work, instead of choosing to stay in and bake and cook some favorite food, deciding to go to the mall may be another kind of fun that may be harmful to the bank account if things are to be bought, but better for the body if the food at the mall is not to be considered interesting, because it wastes a lot of shopping time. **The big thing about this point is that you get to change your lifestyle before you change your eating habits. It's easier than trying to change eating habits while still holding on to the same other habits, behavior, routine, or simply lifestyle.** While most people complain about gaining weight during the holiday season, I complain about gaining weight during summertime. Holidays are not a problem for me because there are only a few holidays in the middle of the cold season. So, I only get to overeat during those few special days. But the lifestyle I lead over summer under the sunshine causes me to overeat more days. The nice weather encourages my family and me to eat out more than any other time of the year. The one-week vacations at the hotels far away from home, and the delicious hotel food, plus the fast fried food I binge on while enjoying a car ride on the way to the far away beach, where I can relax for several hours at a time without physical activities, are the problem. The overeating and inactivity cause me to feel guilty before deciding to cool myself down with the ocean water while diving on the waves, and just like that, the guilt is cleared by that last activity.

While food may be very tempting, **getting out of the food addiction may sometimes mean taking advantage of the situations that discourage you from unhealthy eating.** Such situations may include skipping food that's not delicious, avoiding pushing yourself to eat when you don't have an appetite, and fasting for prayers when church requests members to. Also, avoiding going out of your way to get food that's not currently available, like driving to a restaurant on a super-hot or cold day or driving to the grocery store in order to fix a situation where ice-cream is missing from the freezer, and other such situations are ways to avoid an eating opportunity. Taking advantage of situations that lead to exercise is what we have mostly heard being encouraged. For example, doing the cleaning instead of employing the cleaning lady, walking kids to school instead of driving, parking the car farther, doing the art of cooking instead of eating out, hand washing dishes instead of using the dishwasher, going to the mall or grocery store to shop instead of shopping online and many such choices are good, but also taking advantage of situations that pertain to food intake should not be forgotten.

Preserving food is something that I have learned to do in order to eliminate the urgency to eat it. Sometimes the thought of having the food stay any longer in the fridge may cause me to eat it today instead of tomorrow in order to save it from going bad. After cooking, placing some food in the freezer when I think it is too much is better than putting all the food in the fridge. This really helps me from throwing the food away and it also helps me from gaining weight. It's like I'm putting weight in the freezer for a later time.

As odd as it may be to say, I have realized that I can now tell whether I'm eating too much from how many times per day I have a bowel movement. Usually when I'm eating a normal constant amount of food, I go once, around the same time every day. But whenever I go twice or thrice, then I know that I must have had more food than my normal amount. When I look back, I see that I surely ate more, and I cut down and bring my portion size to normal and my bathroom schedule goes back to normal. Weight comes slowly and goes slowly. So, paying attention to such signals may help me from gaining weight by surprise.

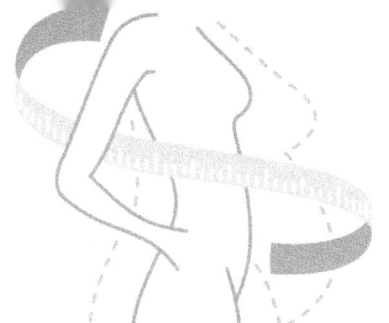

BELLY FAT

Burning belly fat has been the most challenging to me. Right after I got my children, looking at my belly just led to my hopelessness and thoughts of surgical help to get rid of it. If I had the money, I would probably have had a tummy tuck, but I did not have the cash and I'm glad I didn't because I had to do it the natural harder but safer way. Even after months of doing so many ab crunches, working with the ball and running, the belly was still huge. Just thinking how I was going to get rid of it was draining my hope away. The more I worked it out, the more I wanted to give up. One day I went to a party and as I chatted with some friends, one of them said, **"I just think that the best way to get rid of belly fat is to do sit-ups"**. I stopped all other things and started doing 50 sit-ups per day, 4 times a week. For some months I did them and nothing was happening and in fact, the belly even seemed to be bigger, softer, and sagging. I was wondering how come I was feeling all the pain of doing sit-ups and yet I was not gaining any benefits from that pain. Touching my stomach felt as if the fat was broken down for real, but as long as the size of the belly was still the same from outside, I thought I had not achieved my goal. So, I quit doing the sit-ups for about 3 months but to my surprise, within those 3 months, the belly shrunk a great deal. All the broken fat I could feel did not seem broken down anymore but instead, the belly was firming up. I concluded that **when I had done the sit-ups, the belly fat had been broken down but when I stopped doing the sit-ups, the body tried to heal itself from the broken fat and by doing that the belly just shrunk and firmed up.** I have now agreed with the statement that my friend said about sit-ups because I have seen results. I continue to do sit-ups and this time, I am determined not to stop until I shall achieve my goal. In the past, I used to quit exercising the belly as soon as I felt that it had shrunk enough to avoid embarrassing me too much, despite the fact that it had not completely gone. This time I have vowed to myself that I will never stop trying to get rid of belly fat no matter how slowly fat goes.

To this date, if a stranger looks at me, she can still see that I have some belly but for those who knew me when I was bigger, they can say for sure that I have come a long way. I looked pregnant and those who had guts asked me whether I really was pregnant, and that question was a real embarrassment. At least nobody asks me about pregnancy now, and I'm proud of myself for doing that hard work. **If working so hard got rid of the pregnancy question, then I can say I achieved my goal, and my work was worth doing.**

Almost everybody I know who has a belly hates it with a passion, especially women. I have talked to women who are frustrated with their belly, and they just wonder what to do with it. Most of those women are generally heavy but claim that they don't care so much about their weight the way they care about the belly. As for me, I think it is so easy when someone is heavy to work on the belly because they have a chance of losing the belly by just losing their general weight. I try to explain to them that if they diet and exercise, the weight will go and so will most of the belly fat. **There is no possible way of losing weight and leaving the waist with the same circumference as it had before. The whole body changes size, and once the heavy weight is gone, someone can concentrate on working on specific areas in a much easier way. It is easier to do sit-ups when the heavy weight is gone. It would be even better to start working on the belly right away even before losing the heavy weight but what I have seen that idea do to people is just cause despair and hopelessness because it is very difficult to lift one's body in an effort to work on the belly.**

The belly size does not always consist of belly fat only, but a combination of the belly fat and the food, drinks and the gas in the stomach, and all the stuff in the intestines and colon. That's why the belly may appear to be smaller in the morning before breakfast and by the time one is ready for bed at night, it appears to be a whole lot bigger. **By bedtime, how big the belly is depends on how much food and drinks one has**

been consuming throughout the day according to my experience. It also depends on the type of foods and drinks one has been consuming throughout the day since some foods and drinks tend to produce more gas than others. So, if you care about your figure at the party you are going to attend tonight, there is no need to eat beans or such gas producing foods for lunch. What they'll do is cause you to be bloated and make your belly appear to be larger than it otherwise would be.

Sometimes the belly size also depends on how much one has been consuming throughout the week. One day I was trying to decide which dress I was going to wear to a church Valentine's dinner at a 3-star hotel ballroom. I wore the dress one week before the event in order to avoid disappointment at the last minute. One week was enough to allow me enough time to either adjust it or shop for another one. To my surprise, the dress fitted so well except for the belly section. I appeared to be a few months pregnant in the dress and I knew I could not look like that on Valentine's Day if I wanted to feel good. So, I began to cut down the amount of food I was consuming. After just one week, I proudly wore my dress, and the belly was not protruding enough to cause shame. That night, we really had a lot to eat, and I ate until I could not eat any more, but the belly never became nearly as big as it had been one week before the dinner. I concluded that **the belly protrudes more when we eat more, and the more we eat every day, the more the stomach**

expands and demands to be filled with such a large amount of food and drinks as the days go by. That much food and drinks in the stomach expands the belly and causes it to appear larger than it would have been if we had eaten less food. In addition to the fact that the belly appears to be bigger when we eat more, it is obviously true that the actual belly fat under the skin accumulates faster when we eat more than when we eat less and vice versa. **So, eating too much destroys the belly in two ways: it provides the opportunity for the food itself, and the fat it stores, to put a joint effort to push the belly forward.**

As much as we may want to get rid of our belly fat overnight, it may not be possible. Belly fat is difficult to get rid of and as much effort as we may put to exercise, it may only shrink very slowly. But in the meanwhile, life must continue. There is no need to dwell on the size of the belly and let it get in the way of our having fun.

One thing I have discovered that has to be taken into consideration is the size and style of the blouse we choose to wear when the belly is huge. I am very conscious when I buy a top or a dress, but it seems like not everyone is as conscious. It's good to confidently show it all and let it all hang out, but I think it's better to cover it up a little to avoid being conscious of its size and to avoid having other people look at it with questions in their eyes. **Getting a bigger nice flowing top is my secret to hiding belly fat. Avoiding the tops that are short and fail to cover the whole belly is my policy.**

The worst are the tops that have gathers or a belt above the waist because they look just like maternity tops, and they increase the number of months one appears to be far along in 'pregnancy'. Wearing tight jeans pushes the belly way up and creative thinking is required while getting the tops that will not emphasize that upper belly too much. **Most skirts and dresses are better than pants if they are not tight around the hips because they flow all the way down without emphasizing the curve and without pushing the belly upwards.** But that depends on which material of clothes we choose to wear. Some fabrics only make the belly worse than it is by showing the exact curves and the shaking of the belly especially when the clothes are too tight. **To reduce the amount of shaking and to distort the shape of the belly and to make it appear flatter, using proper lingerie may help. Wearing either a cosset or shapewear to hug the belly may improve the experience we have with belly fat. It is universally known that belly fat does not appear to be beautiful, so we might as well take the initiative to hide it while still working hard to get rid of it.**

As much as we may try to hide the belly with clothes, really how much our belly makes us uncomfortable is in our minds. Not too long ago I promised myself to move on with life without caring about the belly too much. The day I stopped fussing about my belly fat is the day I discovered that a big percentage of people have it too. I decided that my belly fat is not going to be the beginning of my fate in fashion and I'm not going to be defined by how big or small my belly is. The only things I have to do are **work on it, dress appropriately, and try to eat right,** but that's as much control as I can have over my figure.

I have admitted that it's natural and beyond our control where our weight sits when we gain it. Others' weight goes to the hips, butt, legs, face, arms or love handles, and nobody gets to choose where they want their weight to go. There is no need for me to sit there and whine about my belly while a big percentage of the people are not perfect either. In fact, I've come to realize that a really good percentage of moms have some belly fat, but since most of them are strange to me and they don't tell me about their discomfort with their belly, I fail to even notice that their belly is a problem to them as much as mine is a problem to me. All I see are people walking confidently without seeming to care about their figure but deep inside them, they may be concerned. I have vowed to myself to walk with my head up without worrying about my belly because I am wonderfully and beautifully made, just like everyone else is, except we fail to appreciate our beauty and worry about it instead of enjoying it. **It's mostly when you complain about your looks that people begin to notice your imperfections.** Nowadays, I don't say anything negative about myself to anyone because I have realized that what you name yourself is what you become even to others. I stopped long ago to ask people, including my husband, what they think about my outfits or my figure. I dress and go.

It doesn't matter what anybody else thinks about what I wear, but my judgment matters most. **I have come to realize that when you ask people how you look, they might take advantage of that opportunity and use it to criticize you. So don't ask. Use your own judgment. Exercise the best you can, eat the best you can, dress the best you can, and then go out there and feel the best you can.** But if you are not trying to exercise, eat well, or dress appropriately, chances are you are perfectly satisfied with your looks and in that case, you have absolutely nothing to worry about. **But complaining about your looks when you are doing nothing to make a change is killing yourself softly. In my opinion, all that complaining will do is lower your self-esteem if it has not done so already.** That is because there is nothing you are doing to give yourself some hope to reduce your imperfections and by telling people about them, you may be hoping for validation, but people may not give you that for many different reasons. Imperfections are okay when they don't bother you, and in that case, you don't have to do anything about them to feel good. **It is when the imperfections bother you that you have to do something about them in order to improve the situation and avoid feeling worse in the future than you do now.**

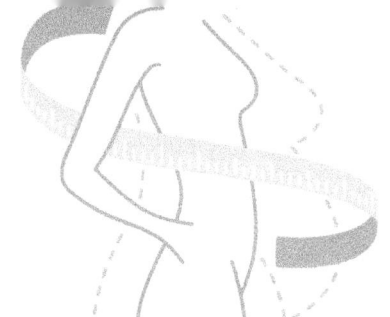

FINAL WORD ON WEIGHT

I would think that weight gain or weight loss is more as a result of psychological problems than anything. Most people turn to food when they are stressed while most others turn away from food. When I was a teenager and stressed, I would turn away from food and I ended up becoming too skinny. In Africa, very skinny women are not considered attractive, or at least that's what I experienced during that time. That's why I never want to lose weight beyond size 8 for the sake of when I go there to visit. During those skinny teenage years, I was really criticized, and the critics were lowering my self-esteem and making me more depressed and more unable to eat, and thus, getting even skinnier. It was a cycle that I imagine goes on with emotional overeaters too. The more they are stressed by some problems, the more they turn to food and the more weight they add. In turn, the more critics they receive, the more rejected they feel and the more depressed they become again, and the more they turn to food again. **I am here to encourage those who turn to food to know that the cycle can be reversed. It only takes a little sacrifice**

of turning to something other than food when they get stressed. It's a sacrifice because the body wants food but it's getting something else. I have come to realize that the mind starts getting interested in something that was initially forced to it. And when the weight begins to go, the more self-esteem one builds, and the less depressed one becomes. As time goes by, this process continues to put one in the right body weight and state of mind. That's what I experienced when I just got my twins. I was feeling horrible inside since my boys were in the NICU, my daughter was living with her aunt for a month and I missed her, and I had the pain of the C-section wound. I turned to the walking program which was very therapeutic to my mind, I started losing weight, got compliments and I felt even better emotionally. I continued with the walking program and started going to the gym to lose even more weight. I got more and more compliments, and the process continued. **My goal is to maintain my current weight to avoid the chances of ever reversing that process that leads to better self-esteem. I have other problems, but when I feel good about my weight, life is not as difficult as it was when I used to feel bad about my weight.**

Weight loss is very achievable. The joy of losing weight is worth the hard work. Mostly, the work is not as easy or as hard as one had imagined. But taking the initiative and beginning this life-changing project is very important. Once started, the project is only good if it's completed. Never quit

along the way. It is better to put the project on hold than to abandon it altogether. The ultimate goal of losing weight is doing just that: losing the weight. If you quit the project, the goal is not achieved. Sometimes we get tired and discouraged, but no matter what comes along the way, it's important not to gain some weight back. If you quit the exercise program, it's important not to quit dieting as well unless you feel sick or unhealthy. Resuming the project is an important step to take to ensure the continuation of the plan. Take it as a marathon. You can slow down along the way, but until you cross the finish line, you have not finished the work you started.

No matter how determined you are during this weight-loss journey, the most important thing to remember is that your health comes first. There are times I would abandon the whole weight-loss plan when I would start feeling unhealthy. I would resume eating like I wasn't trying to lose any weight, and I'd quit exercising. But when I'd feel healthy again, I would resume my project. **I did not quit completely because quitting meant I could not succeed and to succeed, I must not quit. Taking a break for a very long time might lead to quitting. I can't stress enough that taking a break is very important, but it must not mean quitting. I think that it is the guilt of taking a break that partly leads people to quit the plan completely.** This kind of attitude, "I stopped it. Poor me, I couldn't do it", according to me, expresses pessimism, despair, and some guilt. Get over this attitude and realize that at any time you can still get up and begin to change your life. **It is never too late to begin improving your life.** Whenever I do sit-ups, sometimes I start feeling the effect on my C-section inner scars. When that happens, I know it's time to stop. After weeks of taking a break, I know it's time to continue with my project. I don't ever feel guilty for taking a break. My life comes first, then my discipline to keep it healthy.

I also think that when people push themselves to continue the weight-loss plan to a point that they cannot bear it any longer, the conditions turn into torture, and they quit with a never-go-back-there attitude. On the other hand, I think that other people expect it to be so easy that they just cannot continue when it gets just a little harder. I personally know that it is not an easy experience. I get into it knowing that it will seem like torture. That way I expect the worst and prepare for it. The level of torture that I can withstand is relatively high. That is why, from outside, it seems very easy for me to lose weight since I can lose it really fast. But deep inside I know how hard it is to do so. But I am more ready to sacrifice myself than just have it easily. I tolerate the hardships involved in losing weight, and that's almost the main reason why some people can do it fast while others have a hard time doing it. The question is whether you can do whatever it takes to lose weight.

Intense exercise and strict dieting are both relative terms. What I call intense could be mild to someone else and what I call strict could be fair to another. What is comfortable for me as far as dieting and exercising are concerned could be torture to someone else. According to me, whether something is comfortable or torture depends on one's thinking. It's all in the mind. I think the ability or inability to lose weight is more psychological than anything else. For this reason, it is easier for some people to lose weight than for others. That's why I felt compelled to share my experience with those who are determined to lose weight by allowing them into my mind so that they can read my attitude in carrying out the weight-loss project. I hope that I can achieve my goal of getting people to see that it is possible to lose weight no matter what other thoughts cross their minds.

Reading a lot of varieties of sources of information and listening to what people and the media have to say concerning the topic of losing weight is good because knowledge is power. You might know a lot of things but maybe only one thing will open your eyes and help you to achieve your weight-loss goal. I remember one day when I read an article on the internet on how to lose belly fat. Of all the sentences that I read, only one sentence caught my eyes, and it read, "The diet is a must". I was always chasing information on what exercise to do, and I knew dieting is important but the word "must" caused me to realize how important it really is and I began to watch my diet and saw some improvement. Also, when my friend said that doing sit-ups is the best way she believed would reduce the size of the belly, it helped me know for sure that it is important to do sit-ups. How could one person talk about sit-ups so strongly? There must be something good about that kind of exercise. So, I began to do sit-ups, and I saw some improvement. Therefore, **being open-minded is very important because you never know what among all other ideas might work for you.**

The most encouraging thing about doing all the hard work required to lose weight and sacrificing that much in dieting is that there comes a time when all that weight is gone and the freedom to eat returns. I may not eat as much as I used to but just knowing that I have the freedom to go to a restaurant or a party and overeat one time is just freeing enough to eliminate the feeling of guilt and restriction that I feel when I eat too much whenever I'm trying to lose weight when I know I should not be overeating. Surprisingly, when freedom comes, I am usually disciplined enough to just avoid indulging in food unnecessarily. Freedom leads to a good quality of life according to my experience. Maintaining weight for me is easier than losing it. There is a point where eating just enough food will cause the weight to plateau. Most people's weight is on this horizontal point of the line graph where they neither add nor lose any significant amount of weight. I may say that because most people I know have been about the same size for many years and they get to

wear the same size of clothes for years. The clothes may tighten or loosen but the weight bounces between a certain small window. At the dream weight where the weight plateaus, that's the place where the tunnel ends and that's where the light is and that is the place that gives me the incentive to work really hard because once there, there is no more struggling to lose weight, but just watching it. And watching weight is not a big challenge like losing weight. All the torturing exercises and the dieting I go through when I am trying to lose weight are not permanent. After the weight is gone, I can enjoy the foods I missed. For instance, I can sit back and enjoy a piece of cake and some ice cream once in a while. Enjoying it is when I can eat it without feeling guilty afterwards. It's good to know that no matter how much I might choose to eat in one weekend, it's impossible to gain 20 pounds over that weekend. By the time the weekend is over, I'm aware of my carelessness with my diet and I am stopping it without any significant consequences. That's where freedom comes from, facing insignificant consequences and living without the fear of adding weight. That freedom is enjoyable to me. So, it's important to know that there will be a rainbow after the rain. Never quit trying to lose weight based on how hard it is, but rather, get the most serious you can ever be, lose it once and for all and then get comfortable with your newfound lifestyle. Don't dwell on the topic of losing weight all your life.

ENDURING NEGATIVE COMMENTS

We are humans and we are bound to feel hurt when someone says that we are fat. But I have come to know that sometimes **when a loved one comments about our weight, they are just concerned, and they mean to bring this weight issue to our awareness or simply help us realize that our weight is getting out of control, and we need to do something about it.** When I went to Kenya for that weight-loss vacation, my dad and my sister told me that I was big, and it really hurt my feelings. I couldn't understand how my own dad could criticize me like so when he was supposed to be the most understanding of all the people in the World. It was when I lost the weight and went back to Kenya 2 years later that all my relatives and friends commented that I looked good, unlike the last time I had gone there. My aunt even expressed how bad I had looked and how she could not have looked at me without disgust, not believing that I had become so huge and older so quickly. I started asking people why they had not told me that I was big then, and they said that they did not want to hurt my feelings. My dad and my sister said that I looked good with my less weight, and I thanked them very much for letting me know that I had looked fat when everyone else might just have talked about it behind my back. Now I can say that my dad had taken the initiative to let me know that I needed to lose weight because he loves me better than the rest of the world. **I feel compelled to share with you the importance of not feeling bad when family tries to help bring the weight issue to the table because it's only meant to put your mind on the right track concerning your weight.** Remember that even when they don't tell you that you are big, they will think so and sometimes they'll even talk to others about your weight in your absence. **You are the best recipient of this information, and as long as they tell you without humiliating you, I truly believe that they are just trying to show their love to you by suggesting healthy choices. It is better to just do something about the weight than to spend time and energy hurting or complaining about people's comments.** Once you lose weight, you will see how much their comments helped you and you will also see why they had spent their time and energy to comment about your weight.

Weight loss does not guarantee happiness unless one is smart enough to balance all aspects of one's life, I imagine. There are some overweight people who are happier than those with ideal weight. I have heard some experiences of some people who lost weight and lost friends too. This can be more painful than being overweight. **It is very important to treat friendships the same as before the weight loss.** Some people argue that friends who are still overweight are jealous of those who lost weight. To be happy, I would think that you, after you lose weight, have to play your part and leave your friends to play theirs. **If you have managed to lose weight, it's very important to avoid putting down your overweight friends.** Every comment you make to them counts. It's better to encourage them to take the steps you took to achieve your goal rather than criticize them or look down upon them. If your friends feel uncomfortable around you, you are bound to lose them and leave blank the part they played in your life. **Every aspect of life is important, and old friends are mostly better than new ones.** You may gain new friends now that you look better to them and now that you may be more outgoing and confident, but if you lose hurtfully your old friends, you may not be happy. To be comfortable, treat your friends right and let them treat you as they choose, but don't withstand mistreatment either. **If they are jealous and make negative comments, understand their jealousy and guide them with love to understand that you are not pleased with their mean comments.** If you have done nothing to contribute to their negativity other than looking good, chances are it might not disturb you as much as it would if you are the one who provoked them to be so negative. **Avoid what can cause you to feel guilty because guilt can rob you of a great deal of happiness.** I personally would rather be fat than guilty.

Remember that you had the same weight problem for years. You could not resist food, and you could not exercise. So, you ought to be understanding when your friends continue to add weight. Remember all the fun you had dining at different restaurants and talking about food and sharing recipes. The fact that you have seen the light and have chosen to be healthy does not mean that somebody else has. Don't shut them down when they still want to share the food entertainment but **show them in a very kind way that they, too, can choose the healthy path.** Let your health be their inspiration to be healthy. Even when you don't brag, just looking at your new good-looking body might get them to wish that they'd lose their weight too. Never forget that no matter how beautiful you are on the outside, you are better when you are beautiful inside. **If your goal is to attract friendships, you would rather be beautiful inside than outside.**

Sometimes even when you play your part, some people might still make unpleasant comments. For instance, they might tell you that they think you looked better when you were overweight than now. Some may say that to discourage you from doing what you are doing to lose weight because **they are probably jealous,** but others may just not want to see you look different. **Some people don't like to see changes and they would rather see you as they always have than adjust the friendship, they have with you based on your new look.** If, for example you gain more confidence and self-esteem and their confidence and self-esteem remain the same or lower, that means that you no longer sail in the same boat you used to sail in because there is some change in your relationship. Your confidence might be higher than theirs or the same as theirs now unlike before, and the way you have been relating to each other might change. They may therefore prefer to be with people whose confidence and self-esteem have not changed at all and have not changed their relationship either.

It is important to be careful not to get influenced. If you think you look good, nobody else's opinion should matter. One day a good friend of mine commented that I was getting too thin and so I decided to let myself gain weight. About seven pounds heavier, I looked in the mirror and I thought I did not look as good as before that weight gain. So, I worked so hard to lose those pounds I had eaten so hard to gain and I learned an important lesson: I am my own judge. When people would say, "don't lose any more." I would wonder how come they wanted to tell me how much to lose when they were not the ones who got me to lose what I had already lost in the first place. Even when they tried to stop me from losing weight, I still lost more and thought I looked even better. **People never know how you will look like after you lose 10 more pounds until they see you after you have actually lost the 10 pounds.** If my goal was to look as thin as I could comfortably wear a miniskirt or a pair of shorts, they should not have tried to stop me before I got there. Nobody knows what size you want except you, and nobody knows what your fashion dreams are except you. If your dream is to wear a size 8 or 10 skinny pair of jeans, nobody should stop you at size 12. All you will see when you look in the mirror is fat if you don't lose the pounds you want to lose. It's a different case when it comes to people with eating disorders such as anorexia and bulimia. If it's unhealthy, intervention is necessary and should be received positively, but where I come from, size 8 and 10 are not considered skinny or unhealthy.

People will always have something to say about you whether you are fat, medium or thin. So, it's up to you to get the look you want and be happy with it. Don't listen to comments about what hips or butt or burst you have 'unfortunately' lost. We all have different shapes, and we have no control over the proportion of our body parts. Our creation was done long ago, and we did not have a choice of body shapes. It's only better to be content with what we were given and make it healthy, clean and beautiful. We are all beautiful in our own ways.

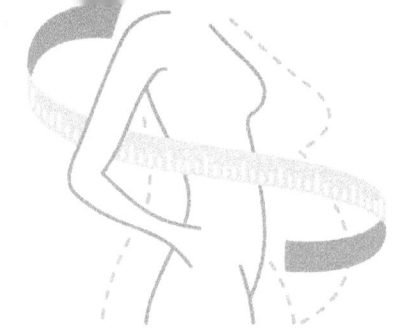

EMOTIONALLY DEALING
WITH WEIGHT LOSS

Losing weight may be one difficult thing but dealing with weight loss emotionally is another thing that may be a big problem too. **Sometimes people add weight as a result of eating a lot and failing to exercise, and sometimes they eat a lot and fail to exercise due to some stress they are going through.** Most of the people I have watched on the screen say that they love food because it's the only thing that accepts them. The food can't criticize them or refuse to be eaten. That food is their best friend, and they always turn to it when they are down. I can really see how it's so easy to turn to food when we are down because sometimes people may be too busy or too selfish to be there for us. Other times people are unaware of what we are going through because we are uncomfortable sharing with them, and sometimes even when we share, they may judge us wrongly and leave us feeling worse than before we shared. So, we turn to some kind of fantasy that will take us away from our stress, and that fantasy may be food, shopping, alcohol, drugs, gambling, sex, or anything, depending on who's choosing what to do. Most of those things we choose to indulge in will eventually catch up with us by having some kind of negative effect on us. Unfortunately, when our fantasy is food, it affects our health and eventually may result in life threatening diseases such as diabetes, cardiac arrest, and others. All these negative effects resulting from some kind of stress that we may have had that led us to eat too much may cause us to realize that those initial problems are really unworthy of worrying about. **But when we somehow manage to lose the weight of our bodies, we may not be able to leave behind the problems that caused us to indulge in food in the first place.** We may be looking good on the outside but inside we may still have the bug that used to bug us. The main difference between now and when we were heavy is that we are healthy, and we feel more socially accepted. We may get as much attention as we may be unable to deal with. Instead of calming down and taking it easy, we may go wild in our minds and do crazy things that we would not have done before the weight loss or before we ever gained weight. Even though we may not choose food again as a way of getting some fantasy, we may choose another addiction such as shopping, parting too much, sex, or anything. One woman I saw on T.V. began to go out with lots of men after she lost weight because she couldn't handle all the overwhelming positive attention she was getting from men. She had been missing it, and all over sudden, she got plenty of it. But the underlying problem that had caused her to gain weight in the first place may not have gone. But this time she wasn't turning to food, but to sex with many partners. That is still a problem, and may cause life threatening diseases, but it's a different problem. **My purpose of writing this section is to encourage those who manage to lose weight to also take time to determine what problem had caused them to turn to food in the first place and to get help in dealing with it.** Losing weight only and leaving the problem unattended may cause us to either go back to food addiction and gain weight again or turn to another kind of addiction, which is not safe either.

The underlying problems that one may be going through could be issues with one's marriage, divorce or breakup, loss of a loved one, bullying at school, failing exams, problems at work, financial problems, or the stress of raising children and overwhelming never-ending house work, all of which may affect one's self-esteem or cause depression. Depending on how one perceives her problem, she may turn to whatever pleases her. It could be food or anything. **If one chooses food to help her feel better, adding weight may be the consequence and being overweight is just a symptom of another problem. So, determining what the underlying problem is may be more important than just worrying about how to lose weight.**

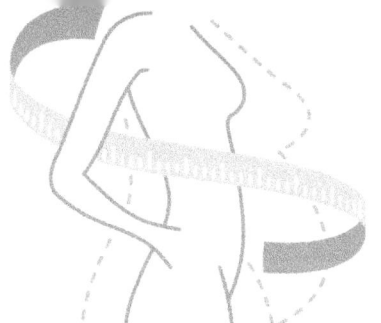

PRESERVING FOOD

As mentioned previously, preserving food is one important measure that needs to be taken in order to help lose weight because it reduces the time urgency when it comes to eating food before we are hungry in an effort to save it. But preserving food is sometimes taken for granted and in the end the food is either over consumed or wasted.

Food is one of the most expensive things, but we may fail to realize it because we only need one plate at a time and one plate is not too expensive, and we always have a place for it in our budgets. There are some people, however, who don't always know where their next dish will come from but somehow, they end up having access to that plate of food or plates for the whole family. My mom has been a farmer for a long time and food was never a problem in our house. Sacks of beans, potatoes, and maize are what I remember used to occupy the food store. Those were grown on a farm in the countryside and after harvesting, they were sold but some were saved and transported to our home. Kales and spinach used to grow in our compound at such a rate that we had surplus to sell. We also had lettuce, onions, and tomatoes growing in the garden. 2 cows mooed with readiness to be milked, and we sold the surplus milk. Then we used the petty cash to buy other foods such as rice and sugar. Sometimes our parents bought packets of wheat flour in dozens, and we got the maize flour from exchanging some maize with processed maize flour for a little fee. We had 7 orange trees in our garden and the ripe oranges were weighing the branches down during the right season. I did not grow up in the country, but all these were in our compound. We had one lemon tree and several banana trees. My parents no longer have all these trees, but they have one avocado tree that drops big avocadoes even on the other side of the fence and passersby collect. We also had chickens that laid eggs, and we could eat the chickens sometimes. We had sheep that my parents could sell and during holidays we ate some as well. We had a drum of molasses for the cows but sometimes we would roll the drum and get a little bit to lick when my parents weren't home. But now I know we were getting some nutrition out of it. We bought a kilo of beef every day. I look back and I surely can see that we had plenty of food.

Some of my relatives came from far to request some of that food and they surely got some. What I used to wonder was what they would do when that food would be gone. But somehow, they managed to do something to feed their families. It is not my own experience that got me to know the value of food, but it's how desperate some of my relatives seemed to be when they were asking to be given something to cook, and how much they said they lacked whenever I was at their homes visiting. I also had other relatives that had plenty and luxurious meals. During meals at their homes, I felt as if I was at a restaurant in a 5-star hotel. I got to experience homes with great kinds of food and homes with little food of less quality.

As much as food is a problem for a lot of people, the same exact people who work so hard in order to get money for food later trash that food when they have had enough for the moment. Knowing very well that in the next 4 hours I will need more food, I don't bring myself to trash good food. I would rather trash other things that I don't know whether I will need in the future or not, but food is a guaranteed need. Sometimes we don't have to wait for the next day to need the food, but we may need it the same day. Some people claim that once they have eaten some food, they can't store it in the fridge to eat it another time. Others say that they can't eat the same kind of food for 2 consecutive meals. All that mentality is in the mind and if the same people would be dropped in a desert with only one kind of food, they would eat it every meal until they would lick their fingers wishing for more. But since we are currently not in a desert and we have options, telling our minds that we can still eat the same kind of food later is all we have to do in order to get ourselves to throw the food in the fridge instead of the trash can.

Storing food in the fridge is one thing and eating it is another. I have realized that some people have a hard time trashing fresh food but when they store it in the fridge, they simply say goodbye to it right then. They don't get to eat that food later and the food goes bad and now they are not guilty when trashing it because it's safer to trash it than to eat it at that point. They cook some more food knowing very well that there is food in the fridge, and then they save leftovers of that new pot and tomorrow they will still cook some more and ignore everything that already exists in the fridge. My secret to avoiding this is to eat what I saved before I cook something new. If what's in the fridge is not enough for the whole family and I have to cook some more, I go ahead and serve and eat the new fresh and hot food but the next meal for me personally will be what I had saved before. Letting it stay in the fridge too long is what gets the mind to dislike the idea of consuming it. But if I stored it yesterday, what mold grow in one day while in the fridge?

The other secret that I have come to learn is the idea of warming the food until it's too hot to even eat, and then letting it cool down a little bit in order to use it. When the food is cold in the fridge, it may look bad and appear not to be delicious. Failing to warm it enough may not bring it to taste delicious because it may have some cold spots. But super-hot food may appear to have come from the pot instead of the microwave. When I was back in Kenya, we never used to have a microwave but now my parents have one.

We would warm food in the pot, and it would boil as if it were being cooked afresh. So, at times even now, when I have to warm a lot of food, I warm it in the pot and when I'm serving it, I feel as if I'm serving freshly cooked food and when eating it, it tastes fresh.

There is one thing I have realized that leads people to ignore the food in the fridge before they end up trashing it: cooking a whole fresh meal without considering what's in the fridge. For example, if I had cooked rice and stew, and the stew is now finished but there is still some rice in the fridge, the best thing I can do is to cook a different stew and use it with the rice that already exists in the fridge. Cooking a whole different recipe of, say, spaghetti and meatballs will cause you to disregard the leftover rice completely and by the time all the spaghetti and meatballs are finished, the rice will be old and will deserve to be trashed.

My husband feels tortured when I take certain measures to control wastage of food. Since he does not like beans and I like to make sure that I don't eat them by myself, whenever I cook rice and beans, **I make sure that I don't cook anything else so that we can all eat the rice and the beans.** Surprisingly, sometimes he goes into the kitchen and makes some stew to eat with the rice and beans. I thought rice and beans were a complete meal but for him it has to have some meat stew. I thought it's good to have grains sometimes instead of meat and that's why I cook them. But I have learned to cook a smaller amount of beans so that they can be gone quickly before they start bringing tension into the house. I may boil a lot and preserve and only fry a little at a time while still cooking other meals in between the beans' days.

Something else that I have been doing when I don't want to eat the same type of food several times in a row is cooking different kinds of food in one day and storing it in the fridge. That way, I can eat rice and stew for lunch, and spaghetti and meatballs for supper. This idea helps to preserve food for those who take offense in eating the same thing two meals in a row. That's because it will discourage them from trashing a certain type of food that they don't want to see later after they've eaten it once. Knowing that they don't have to eat leftovers for supper may put them in a better mood of saving today's lunch leftovers for tomorrow. Even when I don't cook two different meals, I will have, say rice and stew for lunch, and for supper I will find something such as a sandwich, a hot dog, a salad, or anything that I can fix really quickly to help me dodge the rice and stew till tomorrow.

My big thing when it comes to preserving food is freezing the surplus cooked food while it's still very fresh. I go to places for parties and the owners appear to be desperately pushing people to carry food because if they leave it, it will be trashed. When I throw a party and my visitors carry out some, I put the remaining food in the freezer if I think it's too much to be finished in the next 2 days. That way, I don't have to push people who don't want to carry some food to do so, for they may carry it and trash it in their homes if they are the ones that don't like to eat leftovers. Packing food for them is one thing but having them eat it is another. I imagine how I dislike being pushed to carry the kinds of food I don't want to carry especially when the food has potatoes and peas mixed together. Somehow, food with potatoes and peas or spices goes bad faster than most other foods, especially when not properly refrigerated.

When storing cooked food in the freezer, it is very important to divide it into small portions such that it can be used in one meal without remaining. This is because once defrosted, it's not a good idea to refreeze it. Frozen cooked food may go straight to the microwave, but I prefer to place it in the fridge first so that it can thaw slowly before warming it in the microwave or stove. **Warming frozen cooked food too much until it's too hot and then letting it cool down a little is the secret to enjoying it.**

In the freezer, I have ingredients that save me a lot of time when it comes to cooking. For example, when cooking, the part that takes time is preparation of onions, tomatoes, green bell peppers and more of those vegetables that we want to add to our food. Some of those vegetables can be a headache because they go bad quickly and sometimes there is no time to buy them after we've trashed them. **What I personally always do to save my time, and vegetables, is to use a food processor to chop them into the size I want. Then I pack them into sandwich zipper bags and throw them in the freezer.** Sometimes I mix them all up before packing but other times I pack them separately, but I prefer the former option. When it comes to cooking, I grab one zipper bag of my mixture, use scissors to cut up the zipper bag, slide the bag down, get my rock of vegetables as frozen as it is, and throw it in the boiling pot of food. After a little while, it defrosts, and I stir it in the food and wait a little while and then it's all cooked and the food is ready to leave the stove. Sometimes I can fry those frozen vegetables before I add the food, for example when I'm cooking fish fillets. Since the fillets take only a short time to cook and they don't need stirring, it is better to cook the vegetable mixture ahead. But when it comes to beef, I cook the beef first and add those vegetables later to avoid overcooking them. Freezing this mixture of vegetables saves me a great deal of time, money, and health, because it encourages me to cook instead of having thoughts of eating out since it is simpler and cheaper to throw everything in the pot and wait for it to cook than to load everybody in the car and head to a restaurant.

Something else that I benefit from the freezer is storing my children's food. Since I don't like to give them the same meal twice in a row, as they showed me that they don't like it, I have to have different kinds of meals at all times, and they stay in the freezer. **Every time I cook food for the whole family, I pack some little containers of that food and store them in the freezer. Each container is as small as the food can be eaten in one meal by 3 children.** At mealtimes, all I do is grab a container, heat the food, wait to cool and feed the children, and life is good. During the weekend,

I get their frozen fish sticks or chicken nuggets and French fries and bake them, and they get to catch up with their junk food. I can't remember the last time I took them to a fast-food restaurant for a meal, but I have memories of how we used to go there and they would not eat because they wanted to play on the slide. That's how I got discouraged from taking them out to eat but it's now working well for all of us. But once in a while, I still take them to those restaurants to snack and play but not have a serious meal.

Whatever discouraged me from cooking every day was how much I cooked when I was still living at home in Kenya. Cooking and cleaning were like an all-day affair. After breakfast, I used to clean the house and then cook lunch. By the time I was done cleaning the dishes we used for lunch, it was already time to start preparing dinner. Sometimes we would eat late at night because we did something else in the afternoon instead of cooking. Cooking took so much time during those days because of the preparation process. Sometimes it would take going to the garden to get some vegetables before washing them, cutting them, and finally cooking them. Other times it would take going to the grinding mill to get the maize ground into maize meal or exchanged with already processed maize meal before coming home to cook it. Sometimes it would mean going to fetch firewood before coming home to light the fire with which to cook and other times we had to go fetch some water from somewhere whenever there was water rationing. But nowadays there are a lot of prepared foods sold there and all that people have to do is cook it. More people use gas to cook, and they also employ helpers to deliver some water to their homes. Also, more people drive and getting water is not so much of an issue as it used to be. Furthermore, a lot of people have installed big tanks in their homes to store water while a few have drilled boreholes. But all that improvement doesn't mean that some people are not going through the hassle of cooking. Being in America, I have an easier time cooking, but even now, I feel the need to skip cooking some days in order to do something else instead. **Spending all my time in the kitchen is no different from spending all my time doing something else addictive.** The amount of time people spend doing the things they are addicted to takes away the time they could be doing something else that can benefit them in future, and cooking is no different. There will never be a time when cooking will not be done, so we might as well find a way to escape some days of cooking and still avoid going to the restaurants too often to spend money.

When I was a student and single, I did not have time to cook every day and so I would cook a lot of food one day after an exam when I was not in the mood for studying, and I would pack it into small containers and arrange them neatly in the freezer. Days or even weeks later, whenever I would come home hungry, I would warm one container of food, eat it, and go. The food would last long because I was not eating it every day since sometimes, I would eat at school or at work. Even though I am now a mom, and cooking might seem to be my main job, I make sure it is not. Time like this when I'm writing this book could have been the time I could be in the kitchen cooking a new meal if I had trashed yesterday's leftovers. But now I have this chance to inspire others to save food in order for them to use the time they could have used to cook today to do something that may help them or others in future. Sometimes when my husband trashes food, I complain to him, but I don't mention the money he's wasting when he is trashing the food; I mention the time I used to cook that food. And time is money.

While saving food is very important, it is also very important to store food well in the fridge so that we may have more days of enjoying it while it is still fresh. The most delicate foods such as milk, yogurt, eggs and more, are better stored inside the fridge rather than on the inside of the fridge door. I realized that every time we open the door, the food at the door is instantly exposed to the room temperature while the food inside the fridge only receives a fraction of the amount of air in the room and is not likely to warm up as quickly. The farther inside the fridge the food is, the colder it may remain. I used to reach for the milk far inside the fridge at the store in order to get the colder milk and dig in for the eggs that were farther below. Then I decided that it is only fair to take what's in front because if we all avoid what's in front, the products will expire before anybody ever buys them. And if one person does not care to pick what's at the back, he may get a product that has overstayed. But if we all pick what's in front, we'll continuously pick the products as they come, and everyone will share the advantages and disadvantages of doing so.

As much as food needs to be saved, there are things we need to remember. The first thing is that **when food goes bad, it is absolutely unsafe to take the risk of consuming it because there are chances of getting sick from it.** It is better to toss the bad food than to assume that it won't harm you. The money you may be trying to save while eating bad food may be the money you might pay the hospital bill with when you get sick, plus you might not be able to go to work when you are sick, and you may then not make any money either. I learned this the hard way when I decided to take a chance, and I drank some yogurt which I had doubted its freshness. I had never known how slow emergency rooms can be when you are in such stomach pains.

The secret to avoiding eating bad food is to pay attention to the time the food stays in the fridge and to also pay attention to other storage conditions of the food. For example, if you take out food from a restaurant, pay attention to how long it stays in the car before you finally store it in the fridge. Sometimes people leave the restaurants with food, and they pass by other places and the food continues to lose its freshness while in a heated car under the 90 degrees Fahrenheit atmosphere. The car becomes a big oven and continues to keep the food warm. And if the food is fish, shrimp, or other such sensitive foods, it is important to pay attention to its freshness before consuming it. And when it's in the fridge, don't ignore it until one day when you notice its existence and consume it without paying attention. I normally place the old food in front of the fridge and keep the newest food at the back so that every time I open the fridge, I come face to face with the foods that I must eat first. Storing the old food at the back of the fridge may cause you to forget about it until you get a chance to move things around the fridge to see what's at the back.

Also, **failing to keep track of baby bottles may cause problems later.** When children don't finish their milk, they may play with their bottles or sippy cups, and they may later hide them or place them somewhere you may not see. After a few days or weeks, the babies may find those bottles or cups and they may continue consuming their drinks from where they had left. On several occasions, I caught my babies on the verge of drinking bad milk or juice with mold. That's when I learned that I had to make sure that when I gave them a drink, I also had to take the cups or the bottles back. If I couldn't find one of the bottles, then I would have to look for it until I could find it. The milk may be fresh today but poisonous some weeks later.

I've come to realize that in order to prevent an upset stomach and food poisoning, I have to be careful about letting bad food stay in the fridge. I may look at some food and think that it's old and deserves to be trashed but if I don't actually trash it, someone else may eat it or give it to the children. I may be the one who knows how woefully long the food has been in the fridge, but that same food might look like a treasure to someone else and consuming it may cause diarrhea or stomach upset.

In spite of how important it is to preserve food, the most important thing that you have to remember is that **saving fresh food in the stomach is not really saving it.** Eating the whole big plate for lunch in order to avoid trashing the excess does not mean that you will not need supper. You will still end up looking for supper to eat. So, the best thing is to store the food in the fridge instead of the stomach because when it's in the fridge, it can be used for supper or the next day. Once full, there is no need to stuff the stomach because that's the same thing as trashing the food in the trash can. It is actually worse than trashing the food in the trash can because if you trash it, it will not cause you to add some excessive weight. This applies to me too, and I may not point fingers because I have trashed it in the stomach too when it was too delicious. But I have learned that it is better to carry food from a restaurant or party than to eat too much. Carrying it on a plate instead of the stomach is a better choice because you will get to enjoy it later anyway. And later, it may be more delicious, and you'll have saved yourself a lot of discomfort at the party or restaurant as a result of avoiding overeating. **But if food is to be carried away, it has to wait until the next mealtime.** If you carry it from the restaurant and eat it as soon as you get home an hour later, then it will still give you the calories you avoided consuming at the restaurant and you may still need to eat again later during the next meal. In this case, you might as well just have eaten all of it at the restaurant as far as the number of calories is concerned.

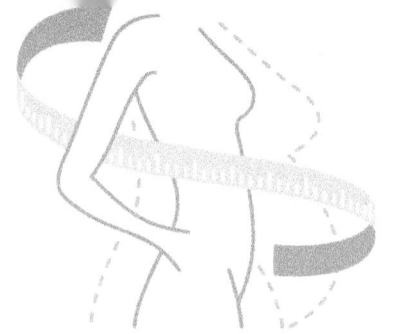

CONCLUSION

Our weight will always fluctuate. I don't know whether anyone can say that his or her weight has been stagnant for years or promise that he or she will maintain the same exact weight for the rest of his or her life. But I know for sure that the most important thing is to never let our weight get out of hand. **If there is anything I would like to encourage you about weight, it's to never give up on it.** That's because the more weight you accumulate, the more discouraged you may become in terms of trying to lose it. And also, it may cause damage to your skin to a point where surgeries may be required to remove the extra skin if you lose weight later, let alone the list of risks that you may be posing to your health during the surgery. **The earlier you begin your journey the better for you in terms of your motivation and success.**

PHOTO ALBUM

Please take time to see the following pictures. Notice the difference between when I was heavier and when I became lighter. Also, enjoy the pictures of my family and get a clue of how my life looked like during the first days of my children's lives. My 'Before Pictures' are pictures of me before I was pregnant with twins, and that's the weight I carried for 3 years. My 'After Pictures' are pictures of me when I had already had my twin boys. In my 'before pictures', I don't have any doubt that I was beautiful, but I'm glad I am not there now since I feel a lot healthier, and I also have an easier time getting clothes to wear than before the weight loss. I used to try on so many clothes before finding one that looked good on me but now, I struggle with deciding what to choose because more clothes look good on me than I intend to buy.

BEFORE PICTURES

AFTER PICTURES

PICTURES WITH MY
DAUGHTER AND TWINS

ABOUT THE AUTHOR

I am a mom of 3. I accomplished a Master of Business Administration in Management from Amberton University, Garland, TX, in 2005; a Bachelor of Science in Accounting from Winona State University, Winona, MN, in 2002; and an Associate in Art and Science from Rochester Community and Technical College in Rochester, MN, in 2000. I attended high school and primary school in Kenya, where I'm originally from. During my school days, the Kenyan education system adapted to the British system of education.

I wrote this book when I was staying at home raising my 3 kids. But currently, I'm an educator. I teach 8th-grade math in Texas. I enjoy my challenging platform as it grants me the opportunity to change the world in a different way in addition to teaching how to lose weight naturally through this book.

www.ingramcontent.com/pod-product-compliance
Lightning Source LLC
Chambersburg PA
CBHW051221120626
46547CB00013B/1450